EILEEN GEORGE:

BEACON OF GOD'S LOVE:

HER TEACHING

EILEEN GEORGE:

BEACON OF GOD'S LOVE:

HER TEACHING

"You will shine as a beacon light before all men,
and you will bring the Father's word to them. . .
A new light has been sent to God's people
and it will light up the whole world."

FOREWORD BY BISHOP TIMOTHY J. HARRINGTON, D.D.

THE MEET-THE-FATHER MINISTRY, INC.

Millbury, Massachusetts

Thanks to Bishop Timothy J. Harrington for his gracious Foreword, and to the Bishops cited in Chapter One for permission to quote them, especially to Bishop Bernard Flanagan. Thanks also to those who introduced Eileen and are quoted. Thanks to Fr. Caldarella and Brother DePorres Stilp, MM for permission to use their articles, to Mother Mary Clare, OSB, for permission to quote from the *Benedictine Bulletin*, to Vivian Warner Dudro for her article in the *National Catholic Register*—and to Father Hugh Nolan for his in the *Catholic Standard and Times*—from which excerpts are taken.

Library of Congress Catalog Card Number: 89–92318
ISBN 0-9624588-0-5 (soft cover)
ISBN 0-9624588-1-3 (hard cover)
Nihil Obstat: Lawrence A. Deery, Judicial Vicar
Imprimatur: Bishop Timothy J. Harrington
October 7, 1989

The nihil obstat and imprimatur are official declarations that a book is free of doctrinal error. No implication is contained therein that those who have granted the nihil obstat and imprimatur agree with—or vouch for the supernatural character of—the contents, opinions or statements expressed.

January   1990   2000 copies
February   1990   2000 copies
March   1990   5000 copies
September 1990   5000 copies

To Mary Who Completes the Mystical Cycle

Contents

PART III
CHANNELS OF GRACE

PART IV
KOREA AND AMERICA

PART V
LAST THINGS

Photographs

Foreword

The words of Eileen George come from her heart and are blessed with simplicity and sincerity. She is an extraordinarily ordinary person, who gives as gifts the gifts she has received. Her credentials are not from colleges or universities but from lived-out, trial-tested, strong, profound faith, hope, and love. Those of us who are privileged to call her friend are in awe of her continual peace of mind and heart, in spite of her personal burden of a terminal illness, and her sensitivity to those who share their woes with her.

Eileen George considers herself as God the Father's child. Her Spirit-filled love for Him and His Son Jesus is a love that is familiar, but rich in reverence and respect.

This book is a compilation of her recorded words. I know she is allowing it to be printed so that her love of God will spread to others.

May that grace be yours . . . and mine.

> The Most Reverend Timothy J. Harrington, D.D.
> Bishop of Worcester

PART ONE

INTRODUCING EILEEN GEORGE

Chapter One

Eileen George's Credentials

(1)

1.1 Eileen George is a very ordinary person, but she is also a very gifted person, equipped for a special mission. We have a right to wonder about these gifts and this mission. However the substance of this book stands on the soundness of the teaching it contains, its correspondence with the teaching of the Gospels and of the Church, and whether it touches the hearts of readers.

This teaching is not presented for the first time here. Eileen has spoken in many places in the United States, Canada and Korea and before large enthusiastic audiences. Thirty thousand heard her in the Olympic Gymnastic Stadium in Seoul in May 1989. Bishops and priests have acclaimed her teaching.

Eileen George often refers to what God the Father or Jesus have said to her. Moreover, this chapter attributes to God the Father certain statements regarding Eileen's mission. These can be skipped by critical readers; they are not essential to the book itself. The question of the source of these statements and of Eileen's teaching is secondary to the teaching itself. The real test of this book of simply expressed doctrine is whether it agrees with the Gospel and moves the reader to draw closer to God. Eileen and her editor gladly leave the final judgment to the Church regarding her teaching and her mission.

Why should these supposed quotations from God the Father be given any credence at all? Like the Gospels, these words can stand on their own, but their credibility has a solid basis. First, what is said of her mission is being fulfilled in fact in one of the fastest growing ministries in the Church. Second, people are brought closer to the Father by Eileen. Third, she leads a simple, unpretentious, eminently Christian life. She is fulfilled in a happy family life as a mother of eight and a housewife. All money received for her services goes not to her, but to the Meet-The-Father Ministry, which is dedicated to the perpetuation of her mission. Having terminal cancer and many illnesses, her ministry is carried out at great personal sacrifice. Fourth, many healings take place through her ministry. "The works I do in my Father's name are my witness" (John 10:25).

The words of the Father about Eileen and her mission come from the year 1982 before Eileen's ministry started. Whence? With two exceptions these were taped by Eileen's spiritual director during her thanksgiving after privately celebrated Mass when she was oblivious of her surroundings. During these colloquies, the Father sometimes asked her to repeat what He had just said. In the two exceptions, the quotations of the Father were made by Eileen herself.

Eileen's teaching, which makes up the substance of this book, are from her public services or from her tapes. Chapter Two explains where she gets the thoughts which she presents.

St. Paul says the Church is built on the apostles and on the prophets (Ephesians 2:20). Vatican Council II recommended that bishops discern charisms, and not quench them. God speaks to us through the teaching authority of the Church, He speaks to us through the Church's scholars whose teaching is in accord with the teaching of the Pope and the Bishops united to him. But He also speaks to us through the prophets, whose teachings support and give life to the Church's teaching. Prophecy does not deal mainly with the future. The prophet is the mouthpiece of God, through whom God gives messages to His people.

(2)
Perceptions of Eileen George's Mission

1.2 The following comments are not simply "testimonials." They tell us about Eileen and her mission, and suggest the geographical extent of her ministry.

THE BISHOPS OF WORCESTER

Bishop Timothy Harrington Introducing Eileen:

(Bishop Harrington, Bishop of the Diocese of Worcester, has known Eileen for fifteen years.)

Tonight we are the witnesses of the power of Christ Himself, pouring out from a woman gifted by Almighty God. That power will, if things happen as usual, most certainly send many away internally at peace and healed, and others healed right in this very spot, and others healed on the way home, or perhaps God willing, by Christmas day.

Nevertheless, healed or not healed, we go away from a person like Eileen knowing God loves us, no matter how frail and weak and fragile we may be. . . . What am I going to say about her that you have not heard? What can I add, except that in my mind she is a faith-filled, loving person and no matter how dreary the day or dark the night she is a person of hope. I say a person singularly blessed by Almighty God. And Eileen will say fast: I am not worthy, I am not worthy. No one of us merits those gifts of faith, hope and charity, nobody earns them, nobody deserves them, they are freely given gifts of God the Father, of the God she calls Daddy, of the Son, and of the Spirit in whose power she relies.

So tonight as you pray for yourselves, pray also for the one here most in need, pray for all the others here, pray especially for Eileen George, because she has been given much, and as Scripture says of those who have been given much, much is to be expected. May she not be found wanting in her return of her giftedness to Almighty God.

Bishop Bernard Flanagan Introducing Eileen:

It's a real pleasure for me to join with Eileen and with you who gather here for this service of teaching and healing. For many long years I have been aware of the many special gifts with which the Lord has blessed Eileen. So when the ministry called now

Meet-The-Father was presented to me during my time as Bishop of Worcester, I was pleased to approve it, feeling very strongly that it would be a means of bringing many of our people closer to the Lord Jesus. And, after all, that is what we are all about in our ministry as priests and bishops, to help the people that we are assigned to serve to draw closer to the Lord Jesus. And I am sure that over the months, through these services that have been held here at St. John's Church, many of our people have felt closer, and in fact have been brought closer to the Lord Jesus.

You are all aware of that beautiful chapter in St. Paul's first letter to the Corinthians, the twelfth chapter, in which he writes about the gifts of the Spirit. He goes on to say that although there is but one Spirit, He distributes His gifts to each individual in different ways. Paul mentions some of them: prophecy, healing, the utterance of wisdom, the utterance of knowledge, the gift of tongues, and the interpretation of tongues. But all these, he says, are the gifts of the one Spirit, and they are given to each of us for the common good.

I think all of us are very much in debt to Eileen for being willing to share the gifts of the Spirit to her, for sharing insights through her teaching, and in many cases her healings, thus helping to bring about a greater love of God in the hearts of so many people bringing you closer to the Lord Jesus.

OTHER BISHOPS

Bishop Hubbard of Albany:

"I have heard many fine and positive things about Eileen's work and I believe that it is a blessing for our diocese to have her come to minister among our own people."

Bishop Robert E. Mulvee of Wilmington:

"Bishop Harrington is a friend of many years. He speaks glowingly of you and the healing ministry and you have my permission to be present here in July."

Bishop Thomas J. Welsh of Allentown:

"It will indeed be a grace for us to have her here again. Please assure her and the Bishop and her Director that she is most welcome."

John Cardinal O'Connor:

"Please assure Bishop Harrington that the Cardinal has been informed of your work, and supports Monsignor Gartland in his intention to bring your special ministry to the parishioners of St. Patrick's [Bedford Village]."

Bernard Cardinal Law:

"Given the soundness of your ministry and its fruit among God's People, His Eminence gladly gives you permission to carry on your ministry in the Archdiocese of Boston."

Bishop Joseph F. Maguire:

"Please know that you have a welcome from me to the Diocese of Springfield. I wish to state in this letter that it will not be necessary for you to request individual permissions. This letter in itself is indication that you are welcome here."

Bishop James C. Timlin of Scranton:

"I hope that you will be able to come and I want to thank you in advance for whatever you can do to help deepen the faith of our good people."

Bishop Thomas Tschoepe of Dallas:

"I have heard from Bishop Harrington, Bishop of Worcester, and he has highly praised the work that you are doing in this area of ministry. We will be most happy to have you here in the Diocese of Dallas."

Bishop Daniel P. Reilly of Norwich:

"I join with Eileen in prayer that the Spirit may enrich with His gifts all who share in this Day of Healing."

Bishop Louis E. Gelineau of Providence:

"I am aware of the great work you are doing in the Diocese of Worcester through the 'Meet The Father Ministry.' I appreciate your willingness to share your talents and gifts with the parishioners of St. Peter's parish."

Archbishop Theodore E. McCarrick of Newark:

"She has the highest recommendation from my Coordinator for Charismatic Renewal. I look forward to meeting her."

Archbishop Roger Mahony of Los Angeles:

"We at SCRC did check your credentials some time ago, including viewing a video tape of one of your healing services. We are satisfied that your ministry is authentic, Catholic and under proper submission to established Church authority . . . Archbishop Roger Mahony has asked that this letter be his own permission for your ministry here."

OTHERS

Father Joseph Pelletier Introducing Eileen's First Service at St. John's Church, Worcester:

"I've had a real sense of expectancy, the Lord is going to do some wonderful things here this afternoon . . . before you go home you will be saying, the Lord has done great things for us, we are filled with joy . . .

"God is a father to us all. Eileen's ministry is called Meet-The-Father. She is starting something new here . . . .

" . . . I'd like you to know that she has had a preaching

ministry for a long time. She has beautiful gifts from the Lord, three of her remarkable gifts are her inspired teaching, her prophetic ministry – she has been giving beautiful prophecies to our prayer group – and the word of knowledge, which is a revelation from the Lord of healings that are taking place. She will use that gift here tonight.

"Though there will be some physical healings here, I am sure the healing we need most and that Jesus wants for us most is spiritual healing, healing of our spiritual sight, and there is no day greater than ours when our faith is so menaced, more weakened by so many things. Our faith needs to be strengthened, and I am sure that the Lord wants to do that for all of us . . . " (*This first monthly service, introduced by Father Pelletier, A.A. a theologian of spirituality, was held October 24, 1982.*)

Appreciation Of Eileen's Ministry in the Philadelphia Catholic Standard and Times, the Archdiocesan newspaper:

"Among the highlights were the faith-inspiring healing services and talks given by Eileen George, the nationally known charismatic speaker. In a personable but compelling way, she asked the people to 'praise and adore God. In this praise and worship, He will fill us with His love and healing power . . . by the time you leave on Sunday, you will know that God the loving Father has truly visited His people.' " (*About the Charismatic Rally Weekend presided over by Cardinal Krol, October 2, 1986.*)

Father Hugh J. Nolan in the Catholic Standard and Times:

"Nearly 200 persons from along the eastern coast under the guidance of the famed Eileen George have completed a five day retreat (July 10–14, 1989), at St. Joseph's-in-the-Hills, in Malvern.

"Mrs. George, who has spoken throughout the world, and who has been invited to China, had just finished conducting a retreat at Anna Maria College and opened the next evening at Malvern.

"Her retreat had been sold out for over four months. Of course, she will go nowhere without the permission of the local bishop, in this case Archbishop Bevilacqua, who was so favorably impressed by her last month at the Charismatic Rally in Villanova, under the able guidance of Msgr. Vincent Walsh, that the Archbishop knelt and received Eileen's prayer over him.

"At one moment deadly serious, at another poking fun at some of the present-day extremes of some so called Catholics (they don't go to Sunday Mass, but go faithfully to a prayer meeting every Monday night) she teaches most effectively the way to the Father, the way to solid sanctity stressing Penance and the Eucharist and the indispensable need for prayer. 'Love is what is needed. If you have the fullness of the Spirit, then you have the fullness of love for everyone.' "

(Father Nolan, pastor of St. Isaac Jogues parish, Wayne, is a frequent contributor to The Catholic Standard and Times.*)*

Msgr. Walsh Of the Archdiocese of Philadelphia, Vicar of Tribunals and of Prayer Groups:

"Once again, the priests at the Philadelphia Conference deeply appreciated Eileen's ministry. An overwhelming majority of the 135 priest participants found time during the retreat to go to her for personal ministry and prayer. At the end of the retreat, many many priests stated that it was the finest retreat that they ever made. This was due to Eileen's ministry as well as to the ministry of the other members of the team.

"For the Youth Weekend, the 155 young adults enjoyed her teachings and the results of the Young Adult Weekend were tremendous."

Father John Wallace, S.M. Introducing Eileen:

"You come here to see Eileen, to be with her and to be touched by her, but, above all, to pray with her, to praise the Lord and to thank Him for His constant love. I know that her great intention is to lead us to the Lord and to prayer to the Lord Jesus every moment of every day. I'd come to hear the Pope, any bishop, any priest, or any lay man or woman who is going to make prayer to the Father through the Lord Jesus in the Holy Spirit more important, precious and valuable.

"Whatever else you have on your mind, whatever healing you seek from the Lord, above all seek this gift, to spend the rest of the month in the presence of the Lord Jesus, until we see her again."

Father Devlin, Principal Marianhill High School, Southbridge Introduces Eileen:

"In the Gospel of Matthew we hear Jesus tell us that if we ask we shall receive . . . I think that when we rest our faith on the words of Jesus and . . . we make them a part of ourselves, then Jesus is welcomed into our lives and He really does great things for us.

"Last August I was sick and I came to see Eileen and I asked her if she would pray with me, and she did. And during the prayer she said to me: 'The Lord will heal you.' And two days later when I went to the doctor, the doctor said to me, 'Well Father that's what I call a miracle!' And so we give thanks to God for the wonderful gift that Eileen has been given to share with each of us.

"We know that God has really blessed Eileen George with a wondrous gift, with many gifts, and we ask her now to come and share these gifts with each of us so that we may give God glory and praise and thanksgiving."

Father Eugene Harrington, S.J. of Holy Cross College:

"I think you'll agree with me on this, that love is like a fire which expands the hearts of men and women. That love is like a fire that inspires men to do heroic deeds. Like a fire, love wishes to spread itself everywhere, and change everything it touches into itself. Love engenders love. This is a good picture of the love of God for us. . . . God is love, God's love was revealed in our midst in this way, that He sent His only Son to the world that we may have life though Him . . . John says: 'Beloved, if God has loved us so, we must have the same kind of love for one another' . . . This is the love that drove Jesus to the cross on Calvary, there on the cross to extend His arms to embrace in love all mankind, everybody, you and me as well . . . and Mary's heart was united with His in His suffering and also in His love for each one of us . . .

"I think this is the love I see, and you see, in our sister Eileen George. Her love for God expands her heart so that it includes everyone. It includes those within the Church and those outside the Church, those in this country and in foreign lands, no matter what the race and creed—her love embraces all. Yet in her heart there is above all the desire that you and I may come to know and realize the love of God for each and every one of us. She wants us to come into an intimate and personal loving relationship with God the Father, in particular, and His Son Jesus Christ. In all her services the Father has blessed us abundantly with all His graces and, for some, even physical cures . . . May the love of God the Father open our hearts, expand them, to receive the message He wishes to give through Eileen—and also the grace to inflame our hearts with love for Him. And so I call now on a true handmaiden of the Lord, Eileen George."

Father Coonan of St. John's Church, Worcester:

"In one short sentence of Chapter 6:38 St. John says: 'The measure you use for others, God will use for you.'

"I think in one word that almost sums up the lady that I am about to introduce today. She gives so much of herself to others, to the Church, to the Roman Catholic Church, as she always says, in a very special way."

Mother Mary Clare, O.S.B., Prioress, St. Scholastica's Priory, Petersham, Mass.:

"Just as the Church has fostered certain missions which have sprung from within her according to the needs of the time (under God always but also mediated through the magisterium), it should not surprise us that God Himself throughout the ages has also given directly to others certain missions for the good of the Church, which the Church not only receives but also, as Hans Urs von Balthasar says, embodies their messages, 'imploring God in the universal holiness of the Church to send more such divine messengers.'

"It seems that today, in Worcester, God has yet again singled out such a messenger to show us how to live the Gospel of love in today's world. She is Eileen George, a wife and mother with eight children. Her message is simple: God wants everyone to realize He is a loving Father to His children on earth; He is caring, tender, gentle. He wants everyone to know of His great love for them; He wants a new world of peace, justice, and love; all who help bring this about will be blessed . . .

"Eileen has an aura of joy and love, and something wonderful, inconceivably beautiful about her. She loves her vocation of wife and mother . . . Eileen is a living witness and expression of the Church's tradition . . .

"And we know that through faith, one reaches a higher and deeper relationship with God than through visions and revelations. But when the latter are given for the good of others and the Church, it would be unfortunate to let negative safeguards always be normative when such safeguards are not called for. Certainly Eileen is an affirmation that prayers are answered by God . . .

"Simple, direct and unassuming as the salt of the earth, Eileen George is a light sent by God to a world that needs yet again to be made aware of His Love." *(From the Benedictine Bulletin)*

The National Catholic Register:

"Throughout salvation history the Lord has chosen the most ordinary people to reveal His power, love and truth to the world.

King David was a mere shepherd boy; Mary, a devout young girl from a small village; the Apostles, 12 unexceptional and uneducated men.

"Modern times are no different. The Lord continues to raise up common men and women to manifest His glory. One of these is Eileen George, a middle-aged housewife, mother of eight children and a cancer patient.

" . . . Since early childhood she has felt close to God, but she did not fully realize His healing power until 12 years ago when she received prayers for severe arthritis. 'I had an inner conviction that I was healed,' she said. 'Five days later I was totally and completely healed.'

"But in 1980 George was diagnosed as having malignant melanoma cancer of the regional lymph nodes. She was given six months to live and suffered through four surgeries. The disease is now in remission. . . .

"Though her presence conveys saintliness, her human warmth and sense of humor would make any sinner feel welcome . . . Her healthy balance of the human and the divine is a living testimony of what it means to be a Catholic."

(From a four column article starting on the first page, June 16, 1985, titled: Mrs. George's Extraordinary Ministry, by Vivian Warner Dudro.)

A Priest Retreatant:

"Eileen, I am now closer to God than ever. I now realize that I never really related to Jesus on a personal level. I, like many other people, put Jesus on a pedestal. We remove Him from being intimate with us. The mystery of the Incarnation is that Jesus came off the pedestal to be one with us so that He could take us to the pedestal. First He had to empty Himself to be a man so that we might become one with God. . . .

"Your relationship to Jesus is beautiful! Sharing your relationship to God with us inspired me to relate to Him on a personal-loving-tender level. For this I will always be indebted. This retreat was the best retreat I ever made . . .

"What I really want to tell you is that my prayer life has changed a great deal for the better . . . What really blows my mind is God's personal tender love that He let's me experience. I have gotten new life from God . . . I am more aware of God's loving presence throughout my day. Scripture and prayer are no longer dry, but exhilarating!

"I still fail at times in really loving my neighbor, but then I quickly become aware of God's grace to love my neighbor and I then try to make amends. I'm more aware of my faults and experience the grace to correct them . . . I am falling madly in love with God!"

Eileen's Spiritual Director:

"Eileen knows Heaven as we know earth!" (*From a two page article about Eileen in the Worcester Catholic Free Press*)

(3)
Dialogue Between Eileen and God The Father About Her Mission

1.3 A Beacon Light Before Men

The Father: "You will shine as a beacon light before all men, and you will bring the Father's word to them. And they will know that you have been lifted up by the Father. A new light has been sent to God's people and it will light up the whole world."

A Fire of Burning Love

"I will enkindle in the heart of My people a fire of burning love, and it will be the everlasting torch, it will burn on and on, and it will be ignited from one person to the other."

Eileen: "Just as You said cancer is spreading throughout the Church, this fire of love for the Father and for the kingdom will spread."

The Father Is Calling His People

The Father: "Eileen, I am calling My people to be holy people, true followers of the beloved Son . . . I am calling you to reveal the Father to all men. This is their last chance. They must listen closely to Your words. The priests must be touched, Eileen. They must realize the great gift of their calling. All this war and heartbreak upsets the Father's heart, yet not as much as the chosen sons. They are crucifying My Son over and over again by their false doctrine, their free living. Eileen, I have placed you upon the earth at this time to work with them in love, not to judge them, but to help them to stand straight and tall. You have a powerful mission, Child, and you must function in this mission to the best of your ability. My graces will be sufficient. Be strong with them, be firm with them, but let them see your love. They must be brought back to the dignity of the royal priesthood. Eileen, this hurts me more than all the trials and tribulations that are to come."

God Is Visiting His People

Eileen: This is the hour to change. God is visiting His people. You may not have another chance. God the Father is saying: "I will visit My people and I will call them together in love, in unity. I, the First Person, will visit My people, and if you don't respond now, there is no one else to send."

If God the Father is coming to visit His people, then we must change, and say: O Father, maybe I haven't been the child you wanted me to be, but help me my Father, by grace, give me a hunger and thirst after the holy life that you have called me to, a hunger and thirst to change. Let it begin with me, not with my neighbor. And let my good example spread throughout my family, my parish, my neighborhood, my business.

The Invisible Trumpet

Eileen: God is calling His people. He is blowing the invisible trumpet that you hear only with the ears of your soul. He says: "Come, come, this is the hour. Because through you, My children, I will renew the face of the earth. Through you, I will bring back the reverence in this Church. Through you, I will bring back your identity as Roman Catholic people, through you, the love of Almighty God will spread."

If we all love one another what a world it would be . . . with love there would be no wars, with love there would be no divorces, with love there would be no abortions, with love there would be no killings. What a wonderful world. So what is the world lacking, my brothers and sisters? The world is lacking love. It is filled with self-centeredness and selfishness, with egotistic people. We are lacking in love.

So what can we do about it? Well the Father is calling you together and He is saying: "I will work with you by grace and acceptance of grace, I will fill your hearts, and I will renew My people."

A Messenger To My People

The Father: "You will rise gloriously as a messenger to My people. They will know that I have sent you. I have raised you up before them. I have gone into the meadow and picked the lowliest of the flowers. And I have set her on a pedestal to shine before all men. They will weep at the sight of her and they will know that I have raised her up to shine before them, and an aroma of love shall flow as sweet honey to their souls, and they will weep, knowing they have rejected her, this messenger of God, this messenger to My people. And when she lies at rest I will flood the earth with graces, graces that have never before and never again will be seen by the eyes of men. A cloud will lower itself to the heads of men and though the sun will shine brightly over the earth the heavens will cry and in the warmest area of My land the snow will fall and in the coldest area of the earth roses will bloom, and the world will know that I have set My flower upon a pedestal and she is coming to Me forever.

Eileen: My Father, I don't understand all Your prose and poetry. I love You, and I feel great peace when You speak such beautiful words to me.

1. Bishop Timothy Harrington and Eileen at her monthly service, December 22, 1985

2. Bishop Bernard Flanagan and Eileen at her service, August 1985

3. Eileen with Mother Mary Clare, O.S.B, Prioress, and sisters of St. Scholastica's Priory

Chapter Two

Eileen George's Mission

2.1 Eileen was chosen by God the Father to bring a message to all people: that He is their real father, loving, gentle, and caring, and that He wishes to be a part of their life. The Father feels keenly the sufferings, frustrations, and disappointments of each of His children. He suffers over their sins, because through sin they drift from Him and harm themselves and others. Nevertheless He does not stop loving them. Human understanding cannot fathom a love so deep and unfailing.

Gradually the Father unfolded the extent of Eileen's mission. Her special intimacy with the Father, Jesus, the Holy Spirit, and Our Lady was given her with a view to bringing many to a similar intimacy with them. Her mission is to the whole world for the present and for the future. The Father has told Eileen that He sent His Son to mankind; He sent His Son's Mother; He sent the Holy Spirit. All have been rejected. The world continues to live apart from the Father, enclosed in its own occupations with very little thought of Him or of its true destiny and purpose. The Father has now no one else to send. So He is coming Himself through Eileen. This is mankind's last chance. The Father wishes to shine through Eileen as a beacon light, leading all to safety in His arms and to a new world of peace, justice and love. All those who help Him in this initiative of love and mercy will be blessed.

2.2 The Beginnings of Eileen's Ministry

Eileen, a housewife and mother of eight, has always had a great reverence for "the royal priesthood of Jesus Christ." Priests began in the 1950s to come to Eileen for advice. They recognized in her a special love and wisdom, and realized that the Father revealed the secrets of their hearts to her.

In 1974 when Eileen joined the St. John's prayer group, she thought that her spiritual experiences were commonplace, and would be experienced by others if they would be sufficiently open to God. She had the gifts of prophecy, revelation, word of knowledge, healing and tongues. Eileen would give a prophecy or teaching from her seat among the others, until she was asked to go to the microphone.

In 1982, the leaders of Eileen's prayer group asked her to give a teaching on "love." Then Father Ray Introvigne, liaison for the charismatic movement in Norwich, invited her to give a healing and teaching service. This was very successful and amazed her friends from Worcester.

In that year, the Meet-The-Father Ministry was formed and presented Eileen in a teaching and healing service on the fourth Sunday of the month at St. John's Church in Worcester at 5:00 P.M. These services continue to the present day, beginning with a priest's introduction and ending with Benediction of the Blessed Sacrament. She has been introduced by Bishop Flanagan and his successor, Bishop Harrington, under whose direct supervision Eileen's ministry functions. Eileen does not accept services unless the group is under a priest. She wishes to be assured that the group accepts the authority of the Church.

Eileen's ministry is one of the fastest growing ministries in the Church. She has given services and retreats throughout the country, in Canada and in Korea to bishops, priests, religious, and the laity. But Eileen has remained a simple, ordinary, home-loving person.

2.3 How the Father's Message is Given

The Father has poured into Eileen's heart a visible love of Himself, His Son, and the Holy Spirit. He wants Eileen to reflect Him and His joy. She often says to the Father, "I want to love You more than anyone has ever loved you. I want all to love You as I love you. But I want to love You the best!"

Eileen leads others to intimacy with God by her prayers, sufferings, example, and teachings. She says, "You may not hear Him as I hear Him, but He will speak to you in the way He finds best for you." Eileen often adds, "He adores you with a small 'a'. " The Father asks that His children come to Him rather than separating themselves from Him by sin and lack of attention. He wants them to love Him, and to receive His gifts and blessings.

Eileen is an example of fidelity to the Three Divine Persons by her love of them and of others regardless of race or religion, by her fidelity to the Church and to the duties of her state of life. Eileen believes that she will be judged on her fidelity as a wife and mother; it is not her gifts which will open the doors of Heaven for her, but only love.

2.4 Eileen, the Church, and Its Teaching

Eileen is proud to be a Roman Catholic; she says, "We have it all." Not that Catholics are all that they should be; she believes that Catholics will only return to their identity when they return to sound doctrine and tradition, and pursue personal sanctification. However, she is not a traditionalist. She accepts the doctrine and discipline of the Church. Eileen believes in obedience; she says that there has never been a disobedient saint and there never will be.

The Father has told Eileen that she will be persecuted, but will not waver from sound doctrine and tradition, nor water it down. She must be an example of courage to bishops, priests, and lay people to encourage them to stand firmly in their faith. Unless they strive to love the Lord with their whole mind, heart, and strength, they will not be able to withstand persecution, which comes also from well-meaning people within the Church. To stand firm, one must think, not of being popular, but of pleasing Jesus. "You cannot serve Jesus and win a popularity contest," she says.

Eileen believes that those outside the Church respect in their hearts those who hold to their Catholic identity. She wants all to know where she stands. She is ready to be of service to all regardless of race, color, or creed, for all are the Father's beloved children. A number of Protestant ministers attend Eileen's services and congratulate her for standing up for the doctrine and tradition of her Church. She teaches that faith is a shield; when a warrior bends too far outside his shield, he is wounded. Eileen applies this to the ecumenical movement; ecumenists should stand firmly in the Faith.

2.5 Eileen's Attitude Towards Her Mission

Eileen leaves the accomplishment of her mission to the Father. She follows the Father's lead, depending on the light and strength of the Holy Spirit. Wrapt up in her love for the Father and Jesus, she is not impressed with herself, rather her greatest suffering is her human separation from Them, imposed by her bodily life. But she enjoys her bodily life. Through it she knows and loves all of the Father's creations, His plants, animals, and especially His children, in whom she finds His reflection. She is a fun-loving person, who enjoys her family life, and is fulfilled in her role as wife and mother. She obtains her husband's consent for her work in the ministry.

This beautiful world is but a pale reflection of the next world. Death will be the doorway to a full unburdened life with the Father, Jesus, the Holy Spirit, the angels, and the saints. Since she has terminal cancer, this full life is not far away – she desires and longs for it. Though she is sensitive to the pain her going will cause her family and friends, she thinks that at the moment of death she will have but one regret: her time for meriting will be over.

Meanwhile Eileen is aware that she must finish the Father's work, including becoming a better person herself, before she can be with Him fully. As she goes on, the veils between her and the Father and Jesus are dropping, but she knows there are many more. Only at death will all these veils fall away in her embrace of Jesus and of the Father.

Eileen sees her gifts not as means to her personal sanctification but for the building up of the body of Christ, to be used faithfully for that purpose. Eileen looks on love – the love of Jesus, the Father, the Holy Spirit, and of all people – as the greatest gift. Her ministry brings Eileen much fatigue, illness, and sleeplessness. Sometimes she leaves on a trip with a 104 degree fever. She constantly has to battle weariness. She considers these conditions the price she has to pay for her ministry. She tells the Father that she will go through any door He opens. He in turn says that He offers the grace to others to open the door to her ministry, but it is for them to accept this grace. He will not invade anyone's free will.

Little things done for the love of God assume a great value in Eileen's eyes: washing clothes and dishes, cleaning her house, baking. She looks for holiness in doing out of love those things which ordinary persons are called to do. Similarly Eileen values the ordinary sufferings and frustrations of life as stepping stones to holiness, not seeking them, but making the most of them by enduring them with patience for the love of God. She believes that these ordinary sufferings: headaches, sleeplessness, mis-understandings, frustrations – and her life is filled with them – may be the equivalent of the "stigmata," as a way of obtaining graces for souls, and much safer. The best way to help people, she is convinced, is through prayer, and offering one's actions and sufferings for them while fulfilling one's daily duties. She teaches that the shortcut to God, Heaven, and holiness, is love. She counsels people to "fall in love with Jesus." This begins the mystical cycle of which she speaks in this book.

2.6 Eileen's Services

Eileen does not know the content of what she is going to say in her teaching service until she speaks. Then it is given her by the Holy Spirit who works through her in accordance with her personality, experience and the lights which the Father has given her and gives as she speaks. Her words, coming from a heart in love with God, inspire love in the hearts of her hearers. It is evident to observers that Eileen does not get her teaching from books or study, but that it is a special gift of the Father for His people. She often says, "No brains, no blockages!"

The second part of her service is a healing service. The Father uses healings to manifest his love and to attract His children to the teaching, just as He did in Gospel times, working healings, small and great, physical, psychological, spiritual, domestic, and financial. Eileen urges those who receive a physical healing to confirm it with their physician and then to come back and give glory to God. She tells them not to discontinue their medications or take off their braces, prescribed by their physicians, but to follow their doctors instructions. She says that God respects the physician's vocation, which comes from Him, and she too respects it.

Eileen's part in these healings is to transmit "the word of knowledge," the word of the Father telling who is being healed of what, and often some of the details, which she makes known to the extent that this will not embarrass the recipient. At a service in Korea in May 1989, Eileen called out a healing of a woman with purple pants. An elderly lady in one of the front rows stood up and pulled up her long white dress, showing her purple pants! The Bishop almost fell off his chair in amazement.

Eileen says that everyone at her services will be touched by the Father, none will be overlooked, they will leave changed. People originally come for the healings; their interest shifts to the teachings, which heal them at a deeper, spiritual level, bringing peace and renewed purpose to their lives. Thus they come to experience the Father's love, and to respond with love to Him. They leave feeling that the Father has truly visited His people. Eileen often says that she is not the healer, Jesus alone is the healer. She says that Jesus honors the expectant faith which people have in coming to a healing service.

2.7 Eileen's Monthly Service

Since October 1982, Eileen has held a teaching and healing service on the fourth Sunday of the month from 5:00 to 7:00 P.M. at St. John's Church, 40 Temple St., Worcester. People come from New England, New York, and Pennsylvania for this service. Sisters, brothers and priests also attend and many of the priests participate in the Benediction of the Blessed Sacrament which closes the service. Audiotapes are available after the service; videotapes, made by Roger Trahan and Paul Tasse, will become available after Eileen's death.

The congregation at Eileen's services are notable for their recollection, good behavior, joy, and enthusiastic praise of the Father and of the Son. They express their delight at the healings by spontaneous clapping in praise of Jesus the Healer and of the Father, the source of the healings.

2.8 Eileen's Priests' Day

Eileen has a Priests' Day from 11 A.M. to noon every second Tuesday at St. John's Church in Worcester. The priests who attend enjoy her teaching, and she is touched by their humility in listening to a laywoman. She says that priests are unique and irreplaceable; they are necessary to the laity and to the Church. Through their words of consecration Jesus comes onto the altar and into the hearts of the faithful and abides in the tabernacle; only through them can the unique healing graces of the Sacrament of Reconciliation be given.

She teaches that priests need to be loved, not judged nor chastised. Good priests will become better and draw others to Jesus.

2.9 Eileen's Background and Sponsors

Eileen was born and raised in Worcester. She attended a public grammar school and a Catholic high school. From the age of 14 to 19 she was a member of a religious congregation, until she was advised to leave because of ill health. She has no theological training, no degree in theology. As a sister she taught in grade schools and attended a normal school for one year. After her marriage she graduated from Bons Secours Hospital School as a registered nurse. She has taught catechism to ninth graders in St. Bridget's parish, Millbury, for about twenty years.

Eileen's services have been sponsored by the Most Reverend Francisco Garmendia, auxiliary Bishop of New York City, by Fr. Ray Introvigne, liaison for the charismatic movement of the diocese of Norwich, by Msgr. Vincent E. Walsh, vicar for charismatic groups and judicial vicar for the archdiocese of Philadelphia, and by other liaisons, pastors and priests.

Eileen has given prophecy at the National Charismatic Rally at Notre Dame to ten thousand people, and has been a principal speaker at various Charismatic Meetings: the New England Conference, the Philadelphia Charismatic Rally, the National Catholic Korean Conference of the U.S., and was invited to Korea for a month by the National Catholic Korean Conference of Korea, ministering there to more than forty-five thousand people in 1986 and to over eighty thousand in 1989.

2.10 Eileen's Cancer

In 1980 Eileen had radical surgery for melanoma of the lymph glands, one of the fastest growing cancers, which is not amenable to treatment. Her prognosis at the time was for six months to two years of life. She was cured a number of years ago from incapacitating osteoarthritis and rheumatoid arthritis which had kept her confined to a wheel chair. She says with regard to her cancer, that while she is not cured of the disease she has the best cure: a happy, joyful heart.

2.11 Eileen and the Meet-The-Father Ministry, Inc.

Eileen is presented in all her services by the Meet-The-Father Ministry, of which she is a member and officer. She has given the rights to all her publications in every form to this Ministry by a legally binding agreement. This is assurance that the works of her teaching in all media will be responsibly transmitted to posterity, which is the purpose of the Meet-The-Father Ministry. While she is unhappy at the thought of being the subject of a biography, she has authorized the Meet-The-Father Ministry exclusively to produce a biography. Eileen receives no personal financial return for her services. The Meet-The-Father Ministry functions directly under the Bishop of Worcester.

4. Eileen about the time her ministry with priests began

5. Joy marks the congregations at Eileen's services.

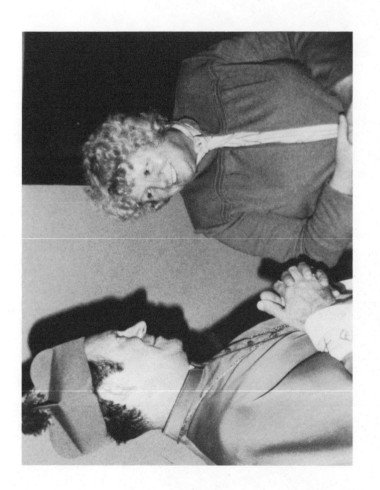

6. Eileen and Bishop Garmendia of the New York Archdiocese

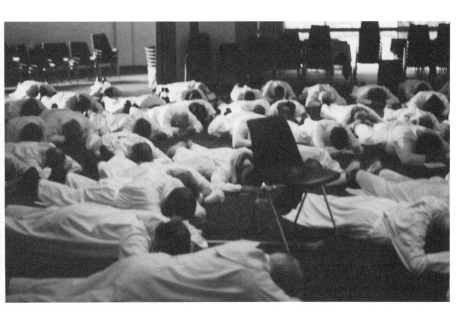

7. Priests renewing ordination promises at retreat at which Eileen preached in Philadelphia; priests at Eileen's retreat in Seoul, 1989

PART TWO

THE MYSTICAL CYCLE

Chapter Three

Father, Son, and Holy Spirit

3.1 The Three Divine Persons

The Father loves you, and He has such a new world to open to you. The Father said to me, "I want you to reveal My Trinity to the people so they can relate to Me." This is my work: to reveal the Trinity in a fuller way to His people. To reveal God the Father, the First Person, Jesus His Son, and the Holy Spirit—all Persons in one God. The Father wants to be loved and He wants His Son and the Spirit to be loved. He wants you to know the Holy Spirit as the Third *Person,* not just as a dove, or a giver of gifts. The Spirit is a Person formed out of the love of the Father and of the Son, the fullness of the love of the Trinity.

In Atlanta, Georgia, as the people were taking me up the Stone Mountain, they wanted me to clarify the Trinity. I was trying to describe it by the triangle: one symbol, three points—one God, three persons. And just as I was explaining it, a beautiful cloud formation appeared shaping a perfect triangle: two narrow clouds coming down from one point and one narrow cloud across. God was confirming it.

When we were small, we were never taught that we had a loving Daddy God. We certainly were not taught about the Holy Spirit. We were taught about Jesus. Now is the hour to reveal each of them and to speak about them.

Even the charismatic people do not look upon the Spirit as the fullness of the love of the Father and of the Son. They rarely ask for the gift of love; they want to be healers. The best gift is love, you can get into Heaven with love. You may not get in with all the other gifts, you may be misusing them.

3.2 The Mystical Cycle of Love

You cannot get to the Father except through Jesus, for so it is written. You cannot get the fullness of the Holy Spirit unless you're led to the Spirit by the Father. You must go through the mystical cycle. The Son to the Father, from the Father to the divine Holy Spirit, and then you can truly say, I live no longer I, it is Christ that lives in me.

Grasp this truth, and let it sink deep within and saturate your soul. Go through this cycle and then you shall see the power of Almighty God working through you, His child. The mystical cycle is a circle of love, peace, and beauty; it is the circle of God's great wisdom. The mystical cycle is man's fulfillment in life.

Hang on to this truth and pass it on to others: there is no other way to get to the Father except through Jesus, and to the Holy Spirit except through God the Father introducing you. Then you will receive the fullness of the Spirit. It is all founded on the love of the Father, being led to the Father, falling in love with the Father, knowing the Father. He is your Father. He'll go to all measures to have you, His child, love Him. You cannot jump over Jesus to get to Him. Hand in hand, Jesus will lead you in love to the Father.

God the Father is not a figment of our imagination or a figment of our faith. He's alive, He's real, and He loves you. He's waiting for you to go to Him. He craves for your love. There is nothing at all that shocks your Father. Go to Him and say, Daddy, or Father, I have this problem or that problem. Together you'll be able to work it out. But how can you work it out, if you do not know the Father? He's a loving Father, He's a gentle Father. Remember this, He loved you first, and He gave his only Son to redeem you so you could get to Heaven. How can you push Him aside?

3.3 He's My Father

When you begin to pray the Our Father, you say "Our Father," He's our Father, given to us by Jesus. He's my Father, mine. God in Heaven is your Father. This beautiful God sitting on the throne, pining for my love, He's God, He's our Father, my Father. How can you not respond to this love? Meditate on these two words, "Our Father." Change it to "my Father." God in Heaven is my Father. He's our Father, that makes us brothers and sisters. We must love one another. Do you see the importance for unity in the words, Our Father?

God is alive, and He's craving for our love. At night, when you rest your head upon the pillow, picture yourself resting your head upon the Father's chest. Feel His loving, protecting arms around you. The Father protecting His child. That's how much He loves you. He sits patiently all day long, waiting for you, His child, to come to Him. Do you go to Him or do you run right by His outstretched arms and cause Him more pain? He's your Daddy, He's your Abba, He's your all.

When you come to the Father, He says, "Beloved, how long I have waited for you, My Child, to come to Me! Many times My arms were extended to you and I saw you running, heading in My direction, but you went right by Me. Is it because you did not know Me? Now that you know Me, come to Me often. I have many things to talk to you about. I have love to give you, and I want your love, the love of a child."

God Almighty is my Father! When you feel yourself tingling with true love for the Father the Father will introduce you to the Holy Spirit. I don't care if you were baptized a million trillion times in the Spirit. Until Jesus leads you to the Father, and the Father fills you with His love, until you truly know there is a Father and you love Him, only then will the Father introduce you to the Holy Spirit. And then and then alone will you truly receive the fullness of the Spirit.

The Spirit will then fill you with love, with fortitude, with wisdom, with miracles, and power, and healing. And greatest of all, He'll kindle in your heart a fire of burning love for your Savior. The Spirit will lead you back to Jesus Christ, Son of God. You'll say at that time, O my God, I never knew it was possible to love Jesus this new and mystical way. You will experience unity, a mystical bond between you and your Beloved Jesus Christ. Then you will feel yourself truly reborn, not in words, but in actions. You'll reflect Jesus. But you have to go through the cycle, there is no other way.

My Father, You gave Jesus to me, so that I could get into Heaven. As I kneel and hug Your knees, Father, I say, I love You so much. Now that I have found You, I will never let You go. Thank You for being so patient with me, thank You for being so understanding of my humanness. Thank You for being our God, but most of all thank You for being my Father, my beautiful, patient, loving Father. I have truly met my Father. I love Him so much, I tingle at the sound of His name. And that's the way you will feel, if you go to the Father through Jesus.

3.4 Turn not your Face from Me

The Father says to you, "My children, My beloved children, I say unto you this day, turn not thy face from Me. I want to see the smile of thy countenance, which reflects the Father's love, and yet day by day, you turn your face from Me. I want to look into your eyes, into the deep pools of innocence. And yet, how often you turn your face from Me. Even though I beckon to you day after day, minute after minute. Do not flee from Me. I have created you, I want to look at you."

I am sure each one of us will say, "But my Father, when do I turn my face from Thee? I do not want to turn my back on Thee, my Father. When do I do this? How do I do this, and why, my Father?"

And you hear Him say, "Child, when you sin you turn your face from Me. When you are unkind and uncharitable to your brother, you turn your face from Me. When you could have done good deeds and yet let them slip away without performing them and instead gave cold indifference, yes, Child, you turned your face. I can no longer see the deep pools of innocence in your eyes, the smile that reflects your father and makes you a child of God. All I see is the back of your head, as you turn your back on me."

3.5 Facing the Father

Far be it from me or anyone of us to want to turn away from the Father. I'm sure each and everyone of us is aware that when we sin, we turn away from God, and that when we are in the state of grace, we are facing God head on. Even though we turn our backs on Him by sin or uncharitableness, by things we could have done and never did, He pursues us. "Here is my grace, turn thyself around and look at Me. Say you're sorry."

But do we accept His grace, are we tuned in to listen to the Father, so we can hear Him say, "Accept My grace by acts of forgiveness, humility, penance, acts of love and charity?"

You see we can be deafened to the voice of God because we are so filled with self-centeredness and pride. These are good earmuffs! So how can we accept the grace He is giving us to turn about face? Instead we turn our face from Him. We must begin each morning by an act of love, and say, "O Father God, I love you beyond all understanding. I want always to be able to look into your Face, in simplicity, honesty, free from sin, my Father. I need your grace to do this. Many times, dear Father, I do have earmuffs of pride, self-centeredness and uncharitableness. Father please remove these earmuffs so I can hear your voice when you call my name." We make so many resolutions, and we fail.

But a humble person is always tuned in to God. Because in their humility they crush themselves, their own desires, their pettiness, and they are facing God head on, as a humble, simple child. When He says, "Here's my grace," they say, "I accept, I thank you, my Father. Father forgive me for I have sinned. I am good for nothing without you, Father. Help me. Set me straight again." Humility allows you to admit and acknowledge your fault, confess a sin, be charitable.

We have to center more on the Father and on the wonderful things He is bringing forth in the world. We should look at Him as a loving Daddy. Father, how wonderful you are, and we are not paying attention. He is doing marvelous things every day. I see it with the birds. One bird will find a new feeder, and before you know it–he must spread the message to all the other birds–there are fifty to a hundred birds at that feeder. God gives the birds and every animal a way to communicate with each other.

We have to take time in our every day life to see what wonderful things our Father is doing. It leaves a deep impression in our souls. Our love will go out to God and looking at His kindness, gentleness and love, His mercy and His forgiveness, we'll not have time for garbage. If somebody is doing all this for you, how can you not have this outpouring love for him?

I used to think, if I do this, O boy, fifty days in Purgatory. That's a cold way to look at God. We're afraid to approach Him. He's aware of our ups and our downs and our good points, but He loves us regardless. He hates the naughty things we do, but He loves us, and there is no limit to His love. So if we take time to seek Him in everyday things our love will be stimulated and will grow.

3.6 The Marshmallow

My Father always treats me with love and gentleness. So I had a hard time relating to the Father in the Old Testament, the fire, the flood, the locusts . . . I'd say, "Gee, Dad, I'm glad I didn't know You then. I'd be scared to death of You."

But one day He told me a story about the Old Testament. "How does the father look at the birth of his son? He swells up with pride, and there is a new kind of love."

I saw it with my own brother. He was a rough, tough Italian boy, and he became a marshmallow with the birth of his son. It was an awesome thing. The Father said, "As Frankie became a marshmallow, when I looked down at my Son, I became a marshmallow."

"Father, You have no weaknesses. How could you become a marshmallow? How could the birth of your Son make you into a cream puff, so gentle, so kind–and no more floods?"

"Eileen, from the beginning of time, I knew this would

happen, so don't think I'm changing. It was always there." And that blows my mind!

3.7 Does God the Father send Suffering?

All along in my walk of life, I hear people say, "Suffering comes from God," "I thank God for sending me this suffering," "Why does God send suffering always to the good people?" "Jesus suffered, so we *have* to suffer," "God sends good things to people, but He also sends bad things." And all of this disturbed me. It blows my mind at times to think that my Father is God, I am His child, He loves me, I can call Him Daddy, my Dad, my own personal Dad. So you see why I get so disturbed over these remarks or when people say to me, "Eileen why has God sent this suffering to you?"

My own earthly Dad loved me very much, as I'm sure your Dad loves you, each one of you. Now my Dad certainly would not have given me suffering, cancer, nor pain, nor would your Dad give you suffering, pain or poverty. I'm sure our Dads want only what is good for us. And they would walk out of their way rather than hurt us. Is God our loving Father, Creator of Heaven and earth, less a Daddy? Does He sends us suffering? No way.

Suffering does not come from God. We are subject to suffering from the Fall of man. Suffering was the consequence of the sin of Adam and Eve. They knew what would happen if they disobeyed. Yet they failed; so this is the consequence. In the meantime God our loving Father sent Jesus to redeem us. Jesus Christ, our loving Savior, the only divine Son of the Father, died upon the cross to win graces for us, to balance the scale of suffering, trials, tribulations, poverty, whatnot.

When suffering does come our way, as it has come my way through cancer, God our loving Father is terribly upset. His heart is aching for me and for His children who are suffering, who hurt. He does not love the suffering–He gives us the graces to bear it, the grace of perseverance in our Faith, and a deep spiritual love, peace, and joy.

Peace and resignation in one's suffering can only come through the acceptance of grace given to us by Almighty God. Who could find joy or peace in suffering? We are only human beings. We hurt, we ache, we bleed. Can we find joy in this? Only by accepting God's grace in this suffering can we find peace, joy, love, so we can radiate Jesus Christ to His Father. He accepts us because He sees His divine Son in us.

I do not go looking for suffering; sometimes I'll walk a mile to get away from it. But since I have been afflicted with this terrible disease of cancer, I can truly say, by the grace of my Almighty Father, I have found joy, peace, and a deeper spiritual life, a love of my Father beyond all understanding. I unite my suffering with the suffering the Father felt when He saw His beloved Son upon the cross. I unite it with His suffering as He sees me, His child suffering. He hurts more than I do, because I hurt and He's my Father.

3.8 When Suffering Comes My Way

No, suffering is not from God, but when it does come my way, He is right there, Johnny on the spot, to give me the grace to bear it, to endure it, to turn it to deep spiritual joy and resignation.

Sometimes when I know I'm going to get a needle, I die a thousand deaths before that needle gets to me. And yet I say, Father God turn Your head away, so You won't see me getting this needle, for I do not want You to hurt, my Father, it's bad enough that I hurt. So you see, if we think more of our Father than of ourself we will find joy in relieving His anxiety about our suffering. There is deep joy and satisfaction in suffering. It is something that you alone have to do, but God's grace is there for you.

Look at Jesus upon the cross. In His divinity He knew His Father, He was the divine Son of the heavenly King. Yet in His humanness, He hung upon the cross. None of us can ever say we suffered as much as Jesus suffered. O no, I'm not going through my suffering alone. I have Jesus and His grace to carry me through.

You know we can turn our sufferings to great joy, into treasures for the kingdom of Heaven, by using God's grace. We can't do it alone, we need grace and Jesus Who is with us in our suffering. We can offer our sufferings up for the salvation of souls, for our own souls, for the royal priesthood of Jesus Christ, as I offer all my sufferings for the royal priesthood of Jesus Christ. Our suffering is a source of great merit. We can become holy as the Father wishes us to become holy, we can be purified by our suffering. We must be purified, and suffering is a sure way of being purified. We can offer our sufferings to our Father God to make up for the sins we have committed. I can accept suffering with joy, peace, and resignation in reparation for all my sins and faults, things I should have done, and didn't do. I will not complain about it.

Suffering is a great treasure, if we accept it the right way. The Father would be so hurt so saddened, if I knelt down and said, Thank you God for this cancer. Instead I kneel and say, O Father God, I know this suffering is not from You, You hurt more than I do, because I hurt. But it's o.k. Father,it's o.k. My body is burning and being purified, and soon my soul will be set free to fly back to You, to be in your arms where it belongs. It's only my body that houses the soul which is burning. Soon my soul will be free, free as the butterflies in the meadow. O, no, my friends, God loves you too much—He's your Father, He's your Daddy, He created you—He does not want you to suffer.

LOVE FOR THE HOLY SPIRIT

3.9 This is a Critical Time

The Holy Spirit must be given His rightful place in the Trinity. This is a very critical time in the Church. Mary is saying it in her apparitions. We can't pass it off lightly. If you don't think so, look around you in the churches. On Christmas Eve and Easter Sunday, there won't be seating for anyone. But those are the only two times you'll see them!

When did the Pope open the Marian Year? On Pentecost, the Holy Spirit's Feast. But we do elbow Him out of everything. God the Father said in 1988, "This is not only a Marian Year, but it is the Holy Spirit's Year. The Holy Spirit must be revealed to My people as the Third Person"– not a dove, not just as power, but as a person . . .

That's what the charismatics forget. They say, Send your power, instead of, Holy Spirit, enter into me, let me be one with you so that I can function in your love, in your light. He is *the Third Person,* and they are not looking at the Spirit as the Third Person. Far too long have we elbowed the Spirit out of the Trinity. And we say, No, no, no, we didn't elbow Him out. O, yes we did. We look at the Father, the First Person. We look at the Son, the Second Person. We look at the Spirit: the dove!

The Holy Spirit is the fullness of the love of the Trinity. God so loved His Son and the Son so loved His Father that this great love they held for each other formed the Third Person of the Trinity, the Holy Spirit. So the Holy Spirit is the fullness of love of the Trinity.

3.10 The Spirit and Mary Go Together

In a parable the Father said to a prayer group, "I have given to you the Third Person, the Holy Spirit and He brings to each and everyone of you many gifts. But if you don't accept Mary into your prayer group, I will withdraw my Spirit and His gifts and He will never come back again."

When Mary was mentioned, the people were saying, This is not a Marian Movement, this is a movement of the Holy Spirit. And the Father was saying, I want Mary and the Spirit to be together, don't exclude either one of them.

The Novena to the Holy Spirit and Parish Renewal

At a Priest Day conference, Eileen said to the priests, Wouldn't it be wonderful, if we could have in the Church the Novena to the Holy Spirit? I feel inspired. I feel that any parish that needs help, no matter in what area, if the people say the Novena to the Holy Spirit, it will help the parish.

The Novena to the Holy Spirit which Eileen says every day, and which she recommends, is published by the Holy Ghost Fathers, Missionlane Building, P.O.Box 2000, Wheaton, Maryland 20902. It is also obtainable in Worcester from the St. John's Prayer Group Bookshop.

Sometimes I feel lazy and say, O, I love to say it, but it's too long. But the moment I pick up the Novena I feel such a tremendous peace. I know that all the gifts that God has given to me for the people come from the love for the Holy Spirit. This love seems to open up all sorts of avenues and doors to a spiritual life. I know I couldn't function without the Holy Spirit.

But we elbow Him out of the picture. We are so human that if we have a devotion, say to St. Thérèse, we think it's all St. Thérèse, nothing else can get in. That's not true with Mary. We must allow space for the Bridegroom to be with His bride, so we can benefit through the Holy Spirit. I do believe we have to get back to some of our old traditions. It's very important. We should hunger and thirst more and more for the Lord. The people are hungry for God. I can tell it on the retreats. At Waltham (January 1988), they were all excited, and were signing up for the next retreat, and they hadn't gone home yet!

We have to look within ourself and find out what we are all about. I don't want you to simply look at the Holy Spirit Novena as a devotion. I want you to look at it as a special grace coming to the parish or the individual. A time for change; a time when you bring in the Bridegroom of Mary into your parish or into your life.

Without the Holy Spirit overshadowing her, Mary would not have conceived. So you see how important the Holy Spirit is. If you say the Novena regularly there will be a change in your life.

THE FALL OF ADAM AND EVE

3.11 You should hear the Father tell the story!

There were two identical trees. From one of these Adam and Eve were forbidden to eat. We call the fruit that grew on these trees apples. When Adam was tempted, he said, 'But the trees are identical!'

Eve who had eaten the forbidden fruit said, 'No, but it is different, I feel different.'

When God came and said, "Adam!" they ran and hid.

Adam said to Eve, "Shhh! Don't answer." This was a doubt that God was everywhere and could see them – the darkness of the mind following upon the Fall. Before the Fall, Adam knew that God was everywhere and that he could not hide from Him.

God called a second time. God was angry and said again, "Adam!" Then they made clothes of leaves because they knew God would see their nakedness. The Father appeared to them in human form to the waist and in great majesty, as the Ruler. The Father said referring to the leaves, "What took you so long and why are you covered? What is this?"

Adam replied, and God said, "How did you know you were naked?" Adam looked at the fruit tree. God, seeing his glance, said, "O, so you ate the fruit!"

Eileen: They are trying to steal away the truth, saying this is a fable. It is true. It really happened.

Chapter Four

Mary

4.1 *John Paul II said about Mary, " . . . when she is being preached and venerated, she summons the faithful to her Son and his sacrifice, and to love for the Father"* (Mother of the Redeemer *quoting Vatican Council II). This is a summary of Eileen's teaching.*

4.2 Mary In My Life

I know with regard to the pursuit of Jesus, many are saying, "Eileen, I cannot make it alone. Can you help me to get to the Bridegroom?" We all need help to find the straight path to the arms of the Bridegroom. And I find the best aid we can have is Mary. Go to our Blessed Mother and lay your cause at her feet. Say, "Mother, I want to get to Jesus, my Bridegroom, show me the way." She answers, "Come, I will lead you to my Son, follow me."

Mary will teach you through humility, for Mary is meek and humble of heart, and her loving task is to lead you to Jesus. She leads you to Jesus through the Rosary, which gives glory to the Trinity. The "Our Father" is there, the prayer which Jesus Himself has given to us. The praise of the Trinity is there: "Glory be to the Father and to the Son . . . " Once you get to Jesus, she will be a powerful intercessor for you to fall more deeply in love with Jesus.

Many of you say, "Eileen, I say my Rosary and do my devotions to Mary." But is that all there is to it? Every Mother wants her son to have a good bride. Mary is the mother of all mothers. She wants you to meet your Bridegroom in the arms of humble love.

Stay close to Mary, pray to her, she wants nothing but the best for her Son, and she'll make you into the best by grace and acceptance of grace. She will groom your soul with all the virtues you need. We must pray to Mary to free us from this pride, this jealousy, this envy that hovers over us. We must pray to Mary to remove any blockages we have.

Say to Mary, "I am far from the best, but by your powerful intercession and grace, I can change this mold of sin which I am, I can get rid of the pride and replace it with humility, get rid of the envy and replace it with charity, get rid of the indifference and replace it with concern. All these things and more you can do for me, Mary. Make me the best. Help me to stay on the true path to Jesus. I need you, Mother Mary."

Be honest with Mary. Humble yourself before the Queen of the heavenly court and ask her to help you. "Change the spots of sin upon this leopard. Help me." And Mary will help you, because you are going to her with honesty and purity of intention. You will be radiant before man, you will radiate the love of God. No matter how old you are, you will be a young bride. And what greater joy to you, the bride, than to have the Mother of God holding your hand and leading you to her Son because now she finds you most pleasing to Him.

Mary does in a sense withdraw once you are with her Son. But she is always in the shadows, watching over you and protecting you, interceding for you. What a joy this is! Do you know the Bridegroom? You have to be honest with yourself. If you knew Him there would be a great change in your life. Has this great change taken place? Don't fool yourself. Mary can intercede for you so that this great change can begin to take place.

4.3 "Hush, Child"

I have loved Mary since I was a little girl. We had a beautiful statue of Mary and a pretty statue of the Little Flower. And although Thérèse was dressed in the handsome Carmelite robe, holding roses, which made her very appealing to a child, I used to look at Mary with such love, and say, "Mary, there is something special about you. I am going to love you the best." I believe with all my heart that that is why I received many graces, many blessings.

One day I was terribly ill, too sick to speak or to move. And in a dream or whatever, Mary was at my side, comforting me, wiping my brow, wetting my lips with her tears. And with unspoken words, I glanced at her in my weakness, and said, "Mary, I should come to you more often. You are the first one to be at my side."

She put her finger to her lips and said, "Hush, Child, my purpose on earth is to lead you to my Son. You are already there."

O the meekness and humbleness of Mary! That doesn't mean that when you find Jesus in a new and beautiful way that you are going to forget all about her, or that she will forget about you. No way! She will be a powerful intercessor as your mother, as your friend, as the Mother of Jesus.

See my friends, we must get our preferences in order. Mary has always been in the background. She wants the limelight for her Son. She says in her apparitions, "Go to My Son. Stay close to Him in the Eucharist."

The Father does not tell Eileen whether Our Lady is appearing in Medjugorje. But He did give her this teaching about the importance of the Eucharist. "Mary has her rightful place in My kingdom. But my children should have their priorities straight. Every morning Jesus is appearing on the altar.

"Everything I give that is good, like T.V., the bad spirit comes in and invades it. I gave T.V. to help make My people holy but also so that they could enjoy it, like the cartoons for the children." And He used the word "cartoon." I think He's hurting terribly. He said, "People who go to Medjugorje come back with a spirit that that's all they talk about."

I go often to Mary. I talk women's talk with her. Sometimes it is easier to talk to a woman than to a man, even though that man be Jesus. I tell her things that are bugging me, things that I want straightened out, and things that I want answers to. And she always helps me, because she is my Mother. She is so interested in my soul.

Maybe sometimes in the different movements of the Church, we excluded Mary through ignorance. But Mary wants to be a great part of our lives, if only we give her a chance. She doesn't want us to adore her, the adoring goes to God. She just wants to be our Mother, to help us to draw ever so close to her Son.

4.4 We have a unique Wonderful Family

We have such a wonderful spiritual family given to us by God: the Father, the Son, the Holy Spirit and Mother Mary. Yet sometimes in our humanness we get all involved with different movements. We call upon the Spirit which is good, but we don't call upon the bride of the Spirit. Remember, she conceived through the power of the Spirit.

We can't separate the Mother from the Son, nor the Son from His Mother. We can't separate the Father from His child, Mary, and we can't separate the bride from the Holy Spirit. As the Spirit overshadows us and give us gifts, and as Jesus comes into the Eucharist, and the Father gives us all things, Mary is there, and she wants to be loved and used by us, to be a part of our lives.

Please draw close to Mary, talk to her, give her a free hand to lead you to Jesus through her intercession. Tell her "Mary, sometimes I *think* I know what is good for me, but, Mary, all the time *you know* what is good for me. So I give you a free hand, groom me as the bride of your Son. Cut, prune, sow, heal. Get rid of any area that will distract me from your Son. Tell the Father of my desires, of my needs. I trust you, Mother."

You see in doing this you are not trying to become pleasing to Jesus the way *you* want to become pleasing to Him. Sometimes our way, in our humanness, is warped. But Mary knows the perfect way to please Jesus. Allow her to be the mother of your soul. Mary will groom you. You will get to Jesus faster and more perfectly.

Chapter Five
The Angels

5.1 Angels are for real, as you and I are for real. They are not fiction. Angels are spoken about throughout Scripture. The Angel Gabriel spoke to Mary. Michael the Archangel cast Satan from Heaven into Hell because he disobeyed God. Frequently Scripture speaks about the angels around the throne of Almighty God. It's not a figment of our imagination. It's not something we tell the kids to keep them happy. It's true. There are angels.

If you could see with the eyes of your soul what takes place during the holy Sacrifice of the Mass! God the Father, sitting on a throne above the priest, watches over His divine Son present upon the altar. All the heavenly choirs of angels are there. If you could hear with the spiritual ears of your soul the melodious tune that the angels are singing during the holy Sacrifice of the Mass! Michael the Archangel is at the priest's right side, protecting the Host that the priest has just consecrated. When the priest gives the blessing, the angels come out over the people and sprinkle them with graces – the only thing I can compare it with is children's sparkle dust – sprinkling graces upon each one in the congregation. That's what's happening during the holy Sacrifice of the Mass. Many people say, If there's no one there I'm not going. Jesus and the Father and the heavenly court with the choirs of angels are there. Our Mass is never dull!

5.2 The Guardian Angels

Each and everyone of you has an angel. And this angel is called the guardian angel. God grants me the grace to see the angel of everyone who comes to me. I believe it's for my ministry. I see the angels bowing to one another, my angel bowing to the angel of the person coming to me, in humble recognition.

When you were in the darkness of your mother's womb, God gave you a present, a gift, your guardian angel. And if anything happens to the child within the womb, if God forbid, an abortion or miscarriage, the angel goes back to the throne of God and bows down. God already knows what happened, but the angel has to give a report to God. And this angel never comes back to earth again. His time on earth is over.

5.3 A Gift, Not a Secret

If my granddaughter had a birthday and I said, Here's a gift, do not open it, that kid would die! She'd be sitting there all day and night wondering what's in the box! Well, God our loving Father gave to each of you this gift of a guardian angel. And He intends you to communicate with this angel, and if you do and you really seek, the angel will reveal himself to you. God did not intend to keep your angel a secret.

Many of the saints saw their guardian angels. Gemma Galgani used to talk and play with her guardian angel. And I know many children have what you call an invisible friend. Can you prove it isn't a guardian angel speaking to this child? If God gave you a present, He wants you to use this present for your enjoyment!

There's no gender in the angels, but when I see a man's angel, I refer to it as "he," and my angel as "she." I've sent my angel on many, many errands. There is something you have to know. Your angel can never leave you to go on an errand. This angel bilocates, trilocates, and multiplies this as many time as our heavenly Father wants, for your use.

5.4 Where are you taking your Angel?

Now if God gave you this wonderful angel, you have to stop and examine your conscience and ask, Where am I taking my guardian angel? Am I allowing my angel to be present in places that are not right before God? Am I bringing my angel into a place where there is liquor and drunkenness? Am I bringing my angel into obscene places? Am I bringing my angel into gossip centers? Where am I bringing this wonderful friend, this wonderful gift that Almighty God has given to me? Just as the angel has a responsibility to you, you have a responsibility to your angel.

I was in the presence of someone speaking slander and off color remarks. And I could see the angel, not moving from the person's side, but shying away from the things that person was saying.

5.5 Hosches in my Ministry

For my ministry, it's important that I see my angel. Every time my guardian angel sees a priest, she (because connected with a female) makes a profound bow to the priest out of reverence and respect. A man with a Roman collar came to one of my services. I didn't know him. I said to my guardian angel, What's wrong with you, Hosches, you're not bowing to this priest? Instead she stood firm and turned. I questioned him, Where are you from, Father? What do you do? And when I searched his soul, because I didn't want him hearing confessions at my service unless he was a legitimate priest, I found out that he wasn't ordained through the right channels of the Church. He gave $25 to someone who ordained him a priest! If he had given him $50 he would have ordained him a bishop. God help us, for a hundred dollars, we would have had another pope!

You see how essential it is for Eileen to communicate with her guardian angel. Hosches made it very obvious to me by not bowing to this person, Look into it, there is something wrong. Never complaining, never accusing, but just suggesting by not making a profound bow. And if there was something wrong, this person should not hear confessions of the congregation. I sent him to the proper authorities and found out he wasn't able to function.

Another time, I was standing up praying over people in St. John's church, and a person came up, so holy, so righteously, powerful it seemed. When she stepped in front of me, the angel shied. And I couldn't understand it. Later on, when we were downstairs in the kitchen area, she would have beaten me to a pulp, if it were not for the presence of a priest. A bad spirit was in her. I asked her to come into that room because my angel turned away from her instead of giving her angel a bow, a little less than profound. The priest was trying to hold her legs down, and she was kicking my shins, giving me uppercuts and spitting in my face. You see how important it is that I can communicate with my angel.

5.6 Relating to your Angel

As I can communicate with my angel, you can communicate with yours, if you want to. God will not force you to have a relationship with your angel. The old prayer is so vital: Angel of God, my guardian, dear, to whom His love entrusts me here, ever this day be at my side, to light and guard, to rule and guide. In your sleep, the guardian angel watches over you and protects you. On the other hand, if the angel is such a service to you, you should understand the duties of an angel.

I was at a prayer group, and a lady gave this testimony, "I thank God I'm here tonight. My guardian angel really helped me. I was going to be late for the service; I came to a red light, and the guardian angel let me slip through." No that wasn't the guardian angel. The guardian angel will not help you to break the rules. If you're going to jump out of an aeroplane without a parachute, the guardian angel is not going to save you. You ask for trouble, and you're going to get it. The angel is given to you by God to protect you against evil spirits, not to let you do crazy things.

I received a teaching on this. I was working with Father Mike Warner in Clinton. I was very close to Father Mike. He asked me to come to his church one day. When I went there, he was in tears. There was a desecration of the Hosts. Some boys broke into the church and threw our blessed Lord, the Hosts, all over the floor, and stole the chalices. I became very angry with Michael the Archangel. I said, "Michael, where were you? Were you sleeping? Why weren't you protecting Jesus in the tabernacle? That's your job, Michael. Where were you when this happened?"

And here's the teaching he gave me:

"Eileen, does God our loving Father interfere with your will?"

" 'Course not, what has that got to do with you not taking care of the Lord?"

"Will I interfere with the will of man? No! Those boys certainly didn't realize that that was the Lord Jesus. If they had understood the divine presence, they would never have done it. They were after gold. They threw the Hosts down, but out of ignorance. God wouldn't interfere with their free will, I will not interfere with their will. But if the evil spirits came from Hell and tried to touch our blessed Lord, I would fight them with my mighty sword."

So you see what he was teaching? I'm there, Eileen, to protect Jesus in the tabernacle from whom? from the evil spirits. And that's what your guardian angel protects you from. And that's why it's so essential to say that prayer every single day, Angel of God, my guardian dear. And if you don't know it, just say, Guardian angel, you're a gift to me from God, walk with me today and protect me from the evil spirits. Say a prayer from your heart. It's the duty of the angel to protect you from evil spirits.

5.7 Angels are Present to Us

The school bus stops in front of my house. My youngest, Kelly and Shane, were small. The school bus driver belonged to the Federated Church in my town. When she stopped to let the children off, she put on the flashing lights, she even put her hand out. And I was on the other side of the street, waiting for them. Now you know that the flashing lights mean to stop. Not only that, she was watching very closely to see if the children passed. The children got off the bus, walked in front of the bus.

And just as they were getting past the bus, a car came speeding by. It would have killed both of my children. The bus driver let out a scream. She saw the coat tails of the children go up and they were yanked to the ground. But she saw no one. Guardian angels, yes. The guardian angels are present to us.

After I had my fourth surgery, I was hungering and thirsting after the Lord. First of all, because I was floored that I was going to die in three or four months. But I had a hunger and thirst for the Lord, and I couldn't get to Mass, And I was in such pain. It was eight o'clock in the morning. My son, Shannon, was in the yard washing his car. My daughter, Sharon, took time off from work and she and my daughter Kathleen, my two oldest, were with me. A knock on the door. And there was a nice looking young man. He said, "I come to give Eileen Jesus." He didn't have a pix in his hand. He gave me communion and he left.

My daughters thought, Gee, he's cute, I wonder what kind of wheels he's driving. So they made a bee line for the window. They went from one window to the other, but they didn't see him. Fifteen or twenty minutes later, my son Shannon came in, and he's whispering, "Mom, where's this guy, he didn't come out, where is he?"

"Shannon, he left half an hour ago."

"Mother, I'm washing my car right by the door, how could he have come out? Did he go out the front door?"

"No Shannon he left by this door."

The girls didn't see him or his car, Shannon didn't see him passing through the doorway. I called up my pastor and said, "Father, this is Eileen."

"How are you, Eileen, I meant to call you."

"Well, you visited me many times."

"Is there something I can do for you?"

"Father, thank you for sending a deacon to me with communion."

"Why Eileen, you know we don't have any deacons in our church."

I thought something new had happened since I was sick. "Did the man tell you his name?"

"Yes, he said his name was Michael."

"Eileen, I believe with all my heart Michael the Archangel gave you Jesus."

I could tell you incidents on and on. One with Betty Lindstrom. When we got to the great Oratory of St. Joseph in Montreal, we were devastated because Mass was just ending. And I was hungering and thirsting to receive Jesus. Betty was besides me. And before I knew it Michael was in front of me. My mouth opened and I received Jesus. Betty didn't see Michael, but she saw me open my mouth and saw the Host placed on my tongue. She was awestruck. And then it blew both of our minds – the priest was looking all over the floor, he thought he had dropped a Host, one was missing from his paten. Even when he went back to the tabernacle, he was still scanning the floor. Is this because I'm holy? No. I have to strive every day to be a good person, as you have to strive.

But I know Jesus is alive. I know He desires to come to me, and I know that Michael the Archangel has the power to bring Him. He's the only angel who has this power. He's not a priest, he can't consecrate. So you see how our priests are treasures. The priest has something Michael doesn't have. Michael can go to the tabernacle and give me a Host. Michael can take a Host from the paten and give me Jesus as he did at the Oratory, but Michael can't consecrate. The power of the priest! I'm telling you these secrets to whet your appetites. I want you to see how much the angels love you, how much the angels want to be a part of each one of your lives.

5.8 Talk to your Guardian Angel

If you call me and say, Eileen, I'm lonesome, it blows my mind. You have a guardian angel. Talk to your guardian angel. Don't elbow your guardian angel out of your life. A guardian angel was given to you by God, to minister to you, to help you, to befriend you.

I have a great love for my guardian angel. Sometimes I send a message to someone through my guardian angel. But I want each one of you to talk to your guardian angel and to depend on your guardian angel. God has given you a gift. Don't insult God by ignoring this gift.

If we knew all the beautiful things that are happening in the Church, we would never say, Eileen, I'm going over to this church or that church, because my church is dead. That blows me away. The Church is very much alive, but you're not tapping the sources, and the beautiful things in the Church. You're looking for an alleluia-raise-your-hands time, socializing, when you should be socializing with Jesus and your guardian angel. We're looking for human relationships, and sometimes it's good, it's very healthy, it's very normal, but not to a point that we always need these human gatherings, and we don't need Jesus.

CANONIZED SAINTS

5.9 The Father just singles people out to be canonized to alert the world to different things. Like the Little Flower. To show the world that you don't have to be a great doctor or theologian, and everything. She was a simple girl.

Chapter Six

Falling in Love with Jesus

6.1 The greatest of all invitations is, Let's fall in love! Christ is asking each and every one of us to fall in love with Him. Does it seem like an outlandish invitation? It is so simple to fall in love, it is natural to love. In our humanness we are made for love, we are meant to express love, to give love, and to accept love. Why are we making it so difficult? Christ puts before us the invitation, Come, Child, let's you and I fall in love! Is it so hard to fall in love with the greatest of all lovers? The Son of the King, Jesus Christ, our love, our all! Why does this invitation shake us?

Perhaps you are saying, I accept this invitation, but how are we going to do this? Well, every love affair has a courting stage and your love affair with Jesus must have a courting stage. And how do you do this? By spending time with Jesus before the tabernacle, quiet moments of love, you and Jesus alone. Going daily to the Eucharist and receiving your lover into your heart. This is intimacy. You are loving, you are hugging each other, you are embracing, you are kissing in the Eucharist.

This is all part of the courting stage. How did you fall in love with your wife, with your husband? You spent time with them, maybe every day, at least several times a week. You found out what they like, and what they dislike. And this love grew and grew the more time you spent with each other. Then it led to marriage.

How do you fall in love with your grandchildren? By watching every day the cute little things they do. You fall deeper in love with these little tykes! Because you spend time with them. Well, it's the same with the Lord Jesus Christ. We fall in love with Him by spending time with Him. In the quiet moments of the day, just sit and say, "Lord, I put myself in Your presence." And think about Jesus. And if you can't, picture yourself spiritually putting your head on His chest and being soaked in Him.

6.2 You Can Become Inseparable

It is impossible to fall in love alone. You need a second party, the lover. You are to love, and be loved by, someone. It can be Jesus if you accept His invitation. Spend time with Him in the Sacrament of Reconciliation, get your soul right before God. Spend time with Jesus in the Stations of the Cross. Kneel or stand before each station, and think of what's happening. Think how much He loved you, and what He went through for you out of a personal love. Your heart begins to swell with love for the Lord Jesus Christ. You would have to be a stoic person not to fall deeper in love with Him.

Many people say, "Eileen, I go to many prayer meetings during the week. I go to Mass once or twice a week. I do enough." All these things are wonderful. But then why do you put Jesus away in a corner and forget about Him? He wants to be brought into every part of your life. Not just your tears, not just for a certain time, and then tucked away. Offer things to Him, laugh with Him, cry with Him, speak to Him. When you love someone you want to speak to them all the time. In their presence you find a rhythm of happiness and holiness.

If you truly love Jesus you want to be with Him all the time, and enjoy this happiness, this peace and unity with Him. He must be a part of every moment of your day and of your night. There is no end to loving Him. I want to be with you, says Jesus, always.

Prayer should go on all day long, and prayer is thinking about Him. No set words. Bring Him into whatever you are doing, your cooking, your cleaning, your office work, your work at the shop, your policeman duties, your fireman duties, your hospital duties, whatever. Bring Jesus into every step you take, into every stitch you take, into everything you eat, the beauty you see, the rain, the sunshine. This is loving Him, this is making Jesus a part of your life.

6.3 A Man's Love for Jesus

"It's o.k., Eileen, for you, a woman, to fall in love with Jesus. What about us men?" The Father has put Mary in your life so you can fall deeply in love with her and run to her. But how can I tell a man to fall in love with Jesus, and here we're fighting homosexuality!

Love Jesus as a brother, as a very best friend. If you fall, or whatever you do, you can run to Him as a friend. You love him, and when you love someone you can tell him anything. Sometimes you're afraid to tell your friend that you slipped in this area. But you never have to be afraid of telling Jesus. He knows it already. He just wants you to say it of your own free will. And that's the love men are to have for Jesus. You can fall in love with Jesus, have very much love for Jesus, a deeper love, so you can run to Him with anything, with temptations in any field. He won't bring it up to you. He wants you of your free will to lay your cards on the table. "I know Lord you understand and forgive me. Help me." Then that love relationship of a brother, of a deep special friend, grows.

6.4 I Have to Work at It

Some people say, "It's all right for you to say this, Eileen. You have this relationship." I work at it. A priest said, "Tell them how you've been sick. Let them know you are human." Of course I'm human. I had the flu for eight weeks. I go to confession every week. I fall. They say, "It's easy for you to love God, you have a close relationship." But I work at it.

I couldn't sleep one night. I said to my Father, "Daddy God, If I'm your kid, how come I can't be as gentle as you? How come I fly off the handle? If I'm your image, why can't I be more forgiving, why can't I be more patient?" Talking to Him builds up your love. You work at your love.

After five years of marriage, you work at your love with your husband and your children. The lovie-kissie business is over, and then the work starts. You cook, you bake. At first my husband used to come in and say, "O something smells good!" Now I say, "Daddy don't you like your meal?" And he answers, "Of course, didn't you see I finished it?" "Well I'd like to hear you say it!" We love each other very much, but we have to work at it. And it's the same thing falling in love with Jesus and the Father.

I made only one New Year's resolution, to love Jesus more and more. If I do that everything else will follow. I will go to daily Mass and communion as much as I can, I will spend love time with Jesus, I will love my neighbor, I will fulfill the duties of my state of life. Rather than making a million good resolutions and then breaking them, which I do, why not resolve to fall more deeply in love with the Lord?

We should grow in the virtues of faith, hope and charity, in humility, meekness and obedience. We must practice virtue. This is not pre-Vatican II. People who say that are misinterpreting Vatican II. A young seminarian told me that they don't teach virtue in the seminary any more. About obedience, they are taught that they don't have to obey if it doesn't give them peace! All the blessings will be there where obedience tells them to be and in doing what obedience tells them to do. To bring forth one's own ideas is good, but then if the superior does not accept them, one should obey. That is what God will bless.

If we are really seeking God in the spiritual things we do, there should be some fruits. If there aren't, we're in trouble. It is not enough to say, "I am going to do these things." Then there has to be an examination of conscience. What am I getting from doing these things? Am I a better person? There should be a change in us. We could have a slip of paper to see if we have drawn any fruits today from these resolutions.

6.5 Unconditional Love

You should radiate Christ to others. Love shows itself, and people should see that you are reaching out with compassion and love. We should be more Christ-like. It's pretty hard for us to love Jesus with our whole mind, heart, soul and body, because we can't see, feel or touch Him. We have to exercise our faith.

But the true way to fall in love with Jesus is to read the greatest book ever, the true love story of Jesus, the Stations of the Cross. Some say, I don't know how to say the Stations. You don't have to know how to do them. Just sit before the station and think what went on in that station, and how much He loved you. It's the greatest love story ever.

And just go from one station to the other. We fall in love with Him – by seeing what He has done for us. Love Him as a brother, as a friend, as a personal companion. The best friend you ever had, the best brother you could ever ask for. He will never turn His back on you. You can tell Him anything and everything. He will never hate you. He will never whisper it to anyone else. It's between you and Him. He will never forget you. He will never stop loving you.

My Father was speaking to me about love. He was telling me how there is the love of a mother and a father, the love of a husband and a wife, the love of children and of friends, all these wonderful different kinds of human love. But then He talked about His love. He made me see that we always love people on condition.

We love our husbands and our wives on condition. You be a good husband, you support me, you don't cheat, I love you. But if you cheat, I don't love you anymore. I'll chastise you, and divorce you and cast you out. People will come to me and say, My son doesn't obey, nor my daughter. I threw them out!

And God says, "Eileen, the Christians are not going to get to where I am calling them to be, to love one another as I have loved them, unless they have the unconditional love of God." And that was the teaching He gave me. If we sin, He hates the sin, if we are naughty, He hates our naughtiness, but He never stops loving us. And until we try this, we are not loving. We have to work at it, and we'll be working at it till the day we die. God says, "Love one another as I have loved you."

He doesn't love us with a condition, He loves us unconditionally. But if we search all our relationships, and I did this, we love with a condition. "You hurt me, you are not my friend anymore." The real Christian love is the unconditional love of God. With that unconditional love comes tremendous forgiveness. We are not even scratching the surface.

I started to get new lights on this unconditional love. And I find even in the Charismatic Movement, and even in the Renew program, we are not seeking this unconditional love. We are still at the level of human love. God wants us to reach out with unconditional love. It's very difficult. A priest said to me, "Eileen, that's hard." You bet your boots it's hard! But that's the love God wants us to have for each other.

You don't like it if your husband cheats, that's awful. You have to sit down and talk about this, and see if you can solve it, instead of running right out to get a divorce. Don't throw your children out, sit down, and try to love them, and make them understand you don't like the naughty things they are doing, but "I still love you. And my love for you will never stop." And until we as Christians get to this, its no use looking to tongues, and prophecy and healings, for the whole foundation is the unconditional love of God.

6.6. Doing What We Can

Eileen's teaching always brings her hearers very simply to the basic way to God. That is expressed by St Augustine in the words, "God does not command the impossible, but commanding, He warns us both to do what we can and to pray to Him for what we cannot, and He helps us so that we can."

Pope John Paul II, recalling the tradition of the Church and the teaching of the Council of Trent, shows the conditions for obtaining God's help:

"The tradition of the Church has constantly taught that God does not command the impossible; but every commandment also carries with it a gift of grace which assists human freedom in fulfilling it. However there is need for constant prayer, frequent

recourse to the Sacraments, and the exercise of virtue."(The Osservatore Romano, English ed., 5-VI-87)

This is also Eileen's teaching. When we pray to God and make efforts, He takes into account our prayer and our efforts. He expects us to use our freedom to do what we can to become better persons, while relying on His help to assist us.

6.7 Openness to all God Wants to Do

The most important thing is to put your soul in the right disposition for everything Daddy God wants to do in your life. Many of you want special graces, special gifts. We're going to throw a wet blanket on that. Let's get rid of everything that *we* want. See if you can follow Eileen:

"Sweet loving Jesus, my Savior, my Love, the divine Lover of my soul, I have many desires, many requests. Lord, put aside all these desires for me. I give You permission in my free will. I want to stand spiritually naked before thee, Lord, and to let Your rain of grace wash me. Lead me in any direction You wish, Lord. All I want to be is the person You are calling me to be. Place upon my heart the grace of openness to anything You want to do in my soul. I praise you, Father, I bless You and I love You."

When there is peace and quietness within us, God can work. He wants to do so many things for each one of us. You know the song, You are the potter and I am the clay. O sure, that's fine, God, You can do anything You want with me, and if I don't like it, I'll tell You off! If I want to go in another direction, I'll pull and I'll tug. And yet we say, You are the potter and I am the clay! Well let's really mean it.

6.8 Face Yourself as Christ would Face You

Face yourself as Christ would face you, and find out what's making you, and me, tick. Are we truly walking in the footsteps of the Lord Jesus Christ? Are we really Christian people, or are we only phoney-baloney raise-your-hand-alleluia people?

We belong to a Charismatic group, Renew group, Marriage Encounter, Cursillo. We isolate that group and think that we have it all, and we don't! You can belong to all the groups you want and still not be walking in the footsteps of the Lord Jesus Christ. And you are called to walk in His footsteps. How? By personal holiness.

I can preach to you until I'm blue in the face, and all you hear is words; hopefully words coming from our Father. The priest can preach to you. But if you don't apply it to yourself, there's nothing we can do. Holiness is something so personal. Loving and falling in love with Jesus is so personal. It's a beautiful kind of love that I want each and every one of you to have.

I want people to say about you, My, doesn't he or she radiate God's love, there's something different about her, about him. And that something different is the love of the Lord Jesus Christ. It's a different kind of love, because it's not a jealous love. If someone looks at my husband with an off-beat look she's likely to get a rap in the mouth from me. See, that's a human love. But I love Jesus so much I want you all to fall deeply and madly in love with Him. That's true love. My husband and I love each other with an earthly love. It really has to be purified. So I want you to understand the different kinds of love, and especially our Lord's love.

6.9 For the Salvation of Souls

When I am in an airplane at night, flying to a place to preach or home, I look out the window and down upon the earth. And I see millions, billions, trillions of lights. Some are red, some are green, some are blue, most of them are yellow or white. And I say, God my Father, I offer to you every light that I see upon earth for the salvation of souls. And I look from one window across the aisle to the other window. I don't want to miss any lights. I want to rake in as many souls as I can to the kingdom of Heaven.

"And what does this mean, Eileen?" First of all it means that God accepts this. He is a great and wonderful God. The intention is there, and He accepts this. And it also means that I'm in constant union with my God. Even when I sleep, I pray. I say to God my Father as I lay myself to bed, Father God, while I sleep I offer to you every beat of my heart, every beat of my pulse, every sigh, every movement, my Father, for the salvation of souls. You have to get in the joyful, loving, prayerful habit of always speaking to God.

When I see the sisters, the priests or the laymen walking up the stairs at a retreat house, I quietly pray, Father, every step they are climbing I offer to You for the salvation of their souls. Never on earth will they know that I am praying for them. But when they get to the kingdom, they will know. You can do this all day long, offering all you see to God for the salvation of souls.

6.10 Simple Easy Ways of Finding God

The Father could save all the souls in the world with the blink of an eye, but that is not in accordance with His justice. He wants us to pray for one another. Taste and see how sweet the Lord is. I tell you these simple, easy things, because it is in a simple way that you will find our God.

We may never be asked to be martyrs. We may never be asked to suffer cancer. He's not asking us to say to a mountain, "Be moved." He's not asking us to be crucified. He's asking us to become holy in the ordinary things of our day. You won't have time for all the garbage of the world, the gossip, the jealousy, the ambition and envy, the anger and hatred and fights. You'll only have time for the Lord Jesus Christ, for Jesus, meek, humble, and forgiving of heart.

You won't be overcome by depression. O yes, depression may tiptoe by you. But you'll have the presence of God, so that you will not be swallowed up by it. Then you are bringing Jesus into every corner of your life. And you are growing. You may not feel it, but you are growing in holiness, in closeness to your Father.

6.11 Forgiving

We find it very difficult to forgive. Being an unforgiving person is a tremendous blockage to our spiritual growth. It closes the door to all the graces that God wants to give us. Not that He'll stop giving us graces, but because of this blockage, we can't accept them. What must we do? We must go to the person or persons who have hurt us, and we must forgive them.

Forgive because the Father forgives. What if the Father held grudges against us! We'd be in an awful pickle. There's one thing that goes over and over in my mind, Forgiving is part of living. If you cannot forgive, there is a part of you that is dying. It can't live, you will not allow it to live, because you are holding to an unforgiving nature. In order to live, you must get rid of this unforgiveness. Then you can grow and grow.

Forgiving is part of living, and living is part of God. If forgiving is not part of living, then forgiving is not part of God. Father God is a kind and wonderful father, a forgiving father. It is very difficult sometimes to say, I forgive you. Just like sometimes it is very difficult to say, I'm sorry. It takes humility to forgive. If you won't forgive, you can be sure there is pride there. Say I'm sorry, or I forgive you.

If countries would say this we would never be at war. If husbands and wives would be forgiving, there wouldn't be so high a divorce rate. If children would tell each other they were sorry, there wouldn't be fights. Admit a mistake, this is humility. And if you won't forgive, you can be sure that pride is at work.

Sometimes someone hurts you, and you say, I'll never forgive that until the day I die. What a terrible thing to say! If God said that to us, we would be cast into the fire of Hell. Who are we not to forgive each other? If God our Creator, Ruler of the heavens and the earth forgives me, miserable person that I am, how dare I not forgive my brother, my sister, or my friend? How dare I hold a grudge? Is this what God wants from you?

Say, I'm sorry, please forgive me, or, I forgive you, I know you didn't really mean it. Forgive! Then you are godlike, a child of God, because you are adopting His forgiving nature. You can only do this through grace. Yes, forgiving is part of living.

Chapter Seven

Loving Jesus through Prayer

7.1 What is Prayer?

What is prayer? Simply speaking to God. Someone said to me, "I speak and I speak, but God doesn't listen to me." He listens to everyone. When you begin to pray, as soon as that word trickles off your lips, God's ears are tuned in to you. He's saying, "My child wants to speak to Me." And He's listening to you, as all good fathers listen to their children.

So none of your prayers are going unheard by God. He's listening to every prayer and answering every prayer—maybe not the way you want it to be answered. I've been praying for years for the megabucks!

As soon as you cry out, "God!" "Yes, Child," He's listening to you. When a younger brother comes to an older brother, he says, "O, don't bother me, I am busy."

"Hey, Mom will you help me with this?"

"When my housework is finished."

"Hey, Dad, how about helping me with this?"

"Son, I have to finish these reports."

So when the big brother is ready, he says, "All right, come on in now." And the little tot runs like lightning to be with the person he or she loves.

But Jesus always has time for us. You say, "Hey, Jesus." He says, "Yes." He never puts us on a backburner. He's always available to us. Shouldn't we run to Him more often? But we don't. You know why? We don't have time for Him; we only call upon Him when we need Him. Is this what friendship is all about? I don't think so. Friendship makes us always available, in the good times, the bad times, the happy times, the sad times. And that's the kind of friend Jesus is to us. And we must learn to relate to Him as this kind of a friend, a pal, a brother, a mystical spouse, the Son of God.

It's time we start relating to Jesus, and finding time for Him. And this time that He expects us to find, we call "prayer time." Prayer time doesn't mean being on your knees. You can be busy around the house or the office or in the yard or garden, or wherever your vocation calls you, and you are talking to Jesus—this is prayer time. It's nice to have a special quiet moment during the day, when you can sit with the Beloved, the Lord Jesus Christ. But every moment of your day should be a prayer time.

I find time for everyone and everything, doctors' appointments and all these other appointments, but I don't have as much time for Jesus. If I can divide my time with everyone and anyone, then why can't I give Jesus, my Love, His share of my time? My whole life is supposed to be dedicated to Him. It's because we haven't learned how to pray, how to share our love with Jesus. Maybe it's the autumn of our lives. Who knows? He says, I come as a thief in the night, you know not the day nor the hour—so maybe it's the autumn of my life, and do I want to stand before Him and say, Jesus, I just didn't have the time?

The holy expectation of Heaven and being there forever! This fire must be enkindled in the hearts of God's children. The joy that He'll be coming one day to claim them, not sorrow because they think it's over. Joy because it's just beginning. Just beginning to live, not exist.

7.2 Help Me, I'm Sinking!

Jesus was walking on the water during a storm. Peter was in the boat with the other apostles. He got out and walked towards Jesus, then started to sink, and called out, "Master, help me, I'm sinking."

You have to give credit to Peter. Even though he started to sink, he called out to the Lord. He had that strength. We must have that strength in our trials, our tribulations, our sufferings, our depression, our dark night, our poverty. We'll have this strength only if we make acts of faith.

Peter had an advantage. Our Savior was visibly present to him. Our faith needs to be stimulated, because sometimes we cannot see, hear or touch the Savior. So we could easily sink and not have the strength to call out to Him. But if we make acts of faith in our life, we will have the strength to say, "Help Lord, I am sinking. I don't want to backslide Lord, help me. I need You at this time of my life, more than I have ever needed you before, please Lord, don't abandon me."

You know we even make acts of faith by the good deeds we do, keeping our eyes centered on Jesus. Somewhere in the Letter to the Hebrews I remember seeing, "Do not neglect good deeds and generosity. God is so pleased by sacrifices of that kind. Obey your leaders and submit to them, for they keep watch over you as men who must render account. Act then so that they may fulfill their task with joy, not with sorrow. For that would be harmful to you, and I do not want anything that is harmful to you" (Hebrews 13:16–18). You see you are doing these good deeds for the love of God, which is an act of faith that God is there. You are fulfilling these good deeds and this generosity for Him.

There are many ways to increase your faith. By acts of faith, proclaiming you believe in Jesus. We need faith to see Jesus in the Eucharist, we need a strengthening of faith. We know there is a heaven. We do not see, feel or touch it, but we believe there is a kingdom and we are going to get there. Because Jesus gave us the "Our Father in heaven hallowed be thy name" we know there is a heaven, but that's faith. You want to be good because you want to please the Father. "Father I know you are my Father though I do not see you." There's an act of faith. You go to confession because you know that your sins will be forgiven, you believe what Scripture says, you stand on His words, "Whose sins you forgive they are forgiven."

7.3 "When You Pray, You Hold Back My Hand"

Everytime I lose my temper I feel terrible. I'm waiting for a chastisement; this has to be rectified; God's going to punish me. He loves me, but He's a just God. And the Father said, "Yes, Eileen, I am a just God, and you should be chastised, but when you pray, you hold back My hand, and there's no chastisement." The power of prayer! That doesn't mean I can go out and blow my top anytime I want. It means I should learn by grace and acceptance of grace to control my temper.

7.4 Prayer and Contemplation

I come in contact with priests and people who go to contemplative prayer workshops. I listen closely to them, and I'm not quite happy. I can see that it is going the wrong way.

My Father says contemplation isn't for everybody. He says that people who still pray out of books, and don't know how to pray from the heart are going to contemplative prayer workshops. The Father said, "If they let me do My work, I would gradually bring them into contemplative prayer. But they are trying to force something."

The Father says it's like Buddhist prayer and transcendental meditation: they are looking for an experience, they are not looking for God. If people will seek personal holiness, the Father will lead them little by little to deeper prayer, but they can't force their way in by a technique, or by looking for an experience. They must seek God in sincerity and truth.

7.5 Valleys and Deserts

God my loving Father has been talking to me for many months about my stage of growth in His love. He's been answering the questions that people ask me. They'll say, "Eileen, I'm always in the valley. I'm tired of being in the desert and being dry in my prayer. I'm tired of depression. I'm tired of trials and tribulations. I want to be high in the Lord, I want to love Him so much."

I listen attentively, and I go to my Father, and I question Him about the valleys, the deserts, and the mountain tops. I said, "Father, You know the secrets of my heart, You know what's bothering me. It seems as though everyone who's really struggling to love You, Father, they are always in valleys, in deserts, slipping and sliding in and out of trials, tribulations. They are very upset and slide into a depression. Father God, why do You deal with us like this? You love us so much and You know how desperately I love You, Father. And yet, I know, I'm in valleys many times. Why is this, Father?"

My Father said, "Eileen, the first thing you must learn, and you must relate to others, is the spirit of trust. You must totally and fully trust your Father. Not only when you're happy and everything is going your way, but even more so when you think you are in valleys, or in deserts, in trials or tribulations. You must have a total trust in your Father, and you cannot receive this overnight, you must work for this Eileen.

"O, I could place a great gift of trust within you, but where would be your merit? You must trust Me and say, Father, I don't feel like praying today, but I love You. I want to pray, so help me through this dry spell. See, Child, you are trusting Me to pull you out of this. You're not trying to do it alone. You're not capable of doing one action alone except by the grace of Almighty God, your loving Father.

"Jesus won these graces upon the cross for you, Eileen. Use them, don't ever abuse them. And ask for the grace of acceptance so you may receive them. When you get to the stage of trusting Me, Child, you will realize that valleys are a stage of growth. When you're in a desert, you are growing.

"You'll say, 'Father, how can I grow in a desert? I'm dry, and I can't pray.' But, Child, you want to pray. So you are calling Me in humility, in love, in trust, and saying 'Father, I want to pray so much.' You are not standing still, Eileen. You are moving; you are begging; you are pleading; you are praying. So you're moving in this valley, or in this desert; you're not just stagnant. You're a running stream, and you will grow, and grow, and grow.

"The most blood you own is in your legs. And if you sit down and become still, the blood will not circulate. If you sit down in a valley and run into despair, or become despondent of grace, you'll not grow. But by calling upon Me, for My help, My blessings, My aid, even by complaining, you are circulating the graces and your spirit is being renewed.

"I am the Lord, and to be praising Me, and feeling My consolation is a gift from the Father. But in this highness, you should receive strength, if its the right kind of highness, so when you are in a valley or a desert, you have the strength to cope with it through God's loving grace."

7.6 The Running Stream

"It's like snow at the top of a mountain. It is giving glory and beauty to that mountain. But if it really has tremendous beauty and gets closer to the sun and starts to sparkle, then it begins to melt. And when it melts, it forms a steady stream running down the mountain and feeding the valley below. So, too, you and your highness in the Lord. If you are really close to the sun, you will become a stream of grace, so that when you run into these valleys, or deserts, you can survive, because you're being fed from the strength you received while you were high in the Lord."

This is one way to check out your highness. Are you high one day and in the pits the next day and seem to have no strength at all? Then your highness isn't the stabilized highness in Jesus Christ and God our loving Father.

7.7 Be Still

Many times when we feel like praying novena after novena, prayer after prayer, rosary after rosary, we do it as a habit. We talk the Father dumb, deaf, and blind and so He has to call us into a valley or into the desert. He is only saying: "Now be still." In plain English, "Shut up and let me love you. Let me speak to you. Come sit in my presence in the silence of your heart."

Do you get the message? Be still. Enjoy your valleys, enjoy your deserts, and let God love you. Let Him put His arms around you and say, "Child, these are our moments together. Come and love your Father in the stillness of your heart. I am lonely. Be still. I will do the talking." Comfort your Father in these valleys, in these deserts. The valleys may be trials, temptations, tribulations. But if you spend your time comforting our loving Father, who hurts more for us than we hurt for ourselves, you'll whisk right through these valleys and deserts.

See, most of the time when we're in the valleys or the deserts, we're thinking of "poor me." "Poor Eileen, look where I am. Where is God?" God is right there, He's with you. He will not let you walk through a valley or through a desert alone. He goes before you, and He says, "Child, hold my hand, I've been this way before." If you take your mind off yourselves and find time to comfort your God, because He wants your comfort, your understanding, and your love, if you look at your valleys and your deserts like this, I guarantee you will be looking forward to valleys and deserts. You'll know you are growing, and not stagnant. Try this in your next valley or desert.

7.8 Are You Still Praising the Lord

It's easy to believe when you're sitting on cloud nine and you're raising your hands and you're an alleluia person and everything seems to be hunky dory. "Everything's going my way. O, thank You God!" You're up there on the mountain, but then, the next day, you may be shot down and walking the valley of trials and tribulations, agony or pain, maybe death. Are you still praising the Lord? Are you still saying, "Jesus, I love You so much." Are you just loving Him at the top of the mountain when everything's going your way? He wants you to love Him in your valleys, in your deserts, in your trials and tribulations, in your cancer, in your illness, in your heartbreak, in the separation by death from a loved one. Can you look towards Him and say, "I love You, Jesus. I don't quite understand this, but I love You."

I received a call from a lady in Canada whose nineteen year old son has been in a coma for almost seven months. She said to me, "Eileen, I can't understand such a hateful, mean God." It broke my heart. I thought I was going to die. I gasped on the phone, "What are you talking about?" She said, "How can a God, who gave us His only Son, forget about my son? How can a God let this young man be in a coma, and not lift it from him." She spoke out of anger, and I could understand her anger, and I don't believe in my heart that God, our loving Father, holds this against her. She was talking out of pain, out of desperation.

It took me almost an hour and forty-five minutes to calm her down and get her back to realizing that God loves her and this boy. I said to her, "Give John totally and completely to our Father. Tell Him, 'Daddy God, I know you love him more than I could ever love him. Take my son and whatever you do, I know it will be the best for him.' " She said, "Eileen, I want to say that, but I can't." But by the time we finished our conversation, she did. I said, "And then, when I hang up the phone, there's going to be a time when you're going to take him back, and you'll even, spiritually, raise your fist towards God. But then you must realize He loves you so much, He gave His faultless Lamb for you."

7.9 She was on Top of a Cloud

I met her about three years ago. She was on top of a cloud. She loved God. She had all kinds of gifts. She was a leader in a couple of prayer groups. She was doing a lot. But since this happened to her son, she stopped loving God, not fully understanding. Her love wasn't the real kind of love. It's easy to say, "I love You, God," when everything's going your way, when there's food on the table and money coming in and no heavy bills to pay and you and your husband are getting along great. But the moment a trial or a tribulation comes, voices begin to rise and frustration sets in. We have to get back to being on an even keel with God first, and then with each other.

We have to get back to knowing ourselves, to looking at ourselves by grace and acceptance of grace and finding out if we truly love Jesus. And if we truly love Jesus, what are we doing that Jesus doesn't like? O, He'll always love us, but I'm sure we have things within us. Do we truly love Jesus so that we hunger and thirst for the Eucharist? And when we receive Jesus in the Eucharist, what do we say? Are we always unloading our troubles in His lap? He accepts us on these terms. Or do we try to bring Him love and consolation? I'm always finding out things about myself. Some things that I don't like too much. But I made a resolution, by the grace of God, that I'll never dump on the Lord again. I'm going to be His consolation here on earth. I'm going to bring Him joy and peace and love.

7.10 Consoling God

In my prayer time, I try to hide from God my suffering, large or small. I know we can't hide anything from God. But I'm going to be His consolation more than ever. I'll be Mary Magdalen for the Father, the Son, and the Holy Spirit. I will wipe and anoint His feet and His brow. I will not cause Him the slightest grief, nor bring Him any misery. I will bring Him joy. And why am I coming to this great conclusion in Lent? Because Lent is a difficult time for me. I walk through a dark night of the soul. I feel the withdrawal of the Father and the Son and my heart aches to be with Jesus. And when He comes back, if He comes back, I'll do nothing but love Him and console Him.

Sometimes I get angry, and I say, "Wait until He comes back, then I'm going to take a 'powder' on Him." And I even say to God, "I love You so much, I don't understand Your love. I could never turn my back on You, Father, and hide on You. How come You love me, and You're turning Your back, and You're hiding on me?" But still He doesn't answer. He keeps incognito during Lent. I say, "When the Father's ready to come back to me with the Son, then I'm not speaking." That's my humanness. "I'll fix You, Father." But you see, I'm hurting. I miss him terribly. When I receive communion, my heart aches for Him. But I want each and every one of you to have your heart ache to receive the Lord Jesus Christ. And you can't have your heart aching for Him, or your soul hungering for Him, if you're not in love with Him. To be in love with Jesus, your Eucharistic King, is a whole new life.

If you have Jesus, and then all of a sudden He doesn't seem to be there at your fingertips, believe me, the emptiness is terrible. It's like being in the bottom of a well, and yelling "Help" and no one hears you. There's a time in my spiritual walk during Lent when I say, "Lord, if you never come back to me, You've showered so much love upon me in my lifetime, I'll nurture on that forever."

7.11 Talking to Jesus

When my granddaughter was four years old, she delighted in riding her swing, and the little horsey that's attached to it. As she was going up and down, her mother and I heard her say, "Jesus, look at me, isn't this wonderful, Jesus?!" And that's what we should say. "Jesus, look at me, isn't this wonderful, Jesus? Do you like this new dress I am buying, Jesus? Do you like this paint for my auto, Jesus, or these new tires? Jesus, do you like this new uniform? Jesus is this a good meal?" You see that's being very conscious of our friend, brother, and mystical spouse, our bridegroom Jesus Christ. We are bringing Him into every part of our lives.

We have lost our simplicity. We have lost our trust, and our understanding. And it's because we have too many blockages. "People will think I'm silly." "Maybe He isn't there." " Would Jesus want me to talk to Him while I'm sewing." "Do you think Jesus would want to talk to me while I am painting the barn?" The answer is, Yes.

We have time for everyone and everything, but no time for Jesus. "O, I give Him time at Mass." Is that enough? How do you expect to fall in love with Him, being with Him for maybe a half an hour or forty-five minutes in a week? How do you expect to understand how much He loves you? He is the Son of the Father. He will sit there at Judgment Day. He died for you. He loves you.

And if He is such an important part of our life, and of our eternity, then why do we elbow Him out of the picture? Prayer groups, rosaries, novenas are not enough! You need intimate time with the Lord Jesus Christ, special moments, all day long, even when you are driving the car.

7.12 Personal Relationship With Jesus

I gave a retreat at Anna Maria, and when I came home from the retreat, one dog, only three months old, was out flat, he couldn't walk. I cried. I said, "O my God, I was out doing your work. Couldn't you take care of this puppy?"

My granddaughter, then 5, came over and put her arm around me, "Nanna, don't cry, I talked to Jesus."

"What did He say, Sammy?"

"He said the puppy is going to walk. Don't cry."

I gave the puppy some medicine and I took care of him, and two weeks later the puppy started to walk. Sammy called, she was camping with her grandfather on the Cape. "Nanna, how's the puppy?"

"Sammy, he's walking."

"God told you he was going to walk, Jesus doesn't lie."

The trust of a child. "Jesus doesn't lie!"

And look at all the promises He gives us in Scripture. "I will never leave you orphans." "No mountain is too high, no depth too deep, I will be with you." "If a mother forgets the babe of her womb"–and most likely she won't–"I will never forget you." He gives us all these promises but we don't trust Him.

You must have this personal relationship with the Lord to trust. Get back to that personal relationship with Jesus. All He's asking you to do is to go on a honeymoon with Him. He's inviting you into the bridal chambers of the Eucharist, where you'll have strength.

7.13 Not Feeling God's Presence, Yet He is There

You come to me and say, "God is not with me. God has turned His back on me." This is not true. I know without a doubt that none of you has ever walked through the agonizing pain of the loss of God. The greatest pain in Hell is the loss of the presence of God, God is not there. That's the agonizing torture. And I'm sure God our loving Father allowed me to feel this, so that I can tell you, yes, God is with each one of you.

Even if you don't feel His presence or hear His voice I want you to realize God our loving Father is with you. Until you feel this agonizing pain, and I'm sure you will never feel it on earth, you'll know your loving Father is present. Don't insult Him by saying, God is not with me, He doesn't love me, I don't feel His presence. You feel His presence, you just don't recognize it. All through Scripture He gives you the promises that He'll be with you, holding you, and loving you. Did He not give you Jesus in the Eucharist and in the tabernacle?

I know God only let me enter those gates and feel the terrible pain of loss so I can give this message to you. Yes, He is with you, even if you don't feel His presence. Feelings don't count, God is with you, for if He wasn't with you that agonizing pain would be there and you would die. And that's how I felt, O my God, if I don't get out of here I'm going to die. That's what I want you to realize. Hell, yes, there is a Hell. But more than ever God is with each one of us, if He were not we couldn't breathe or walk or survive, the pain would be so acute.

You want to feel Him in a different way, and He understands that. Draw close to Him and He'll allow you to walk on a different path. He loves you so much. He delights to be with you. He delights to have you speak to Him, to call Him Daddy, to spiritually climb into His arms and say, "Daddy hold me, love me, never let me go."

You see that's what a deep prayer life does for each one of us, myself included. It makes us realize that we are gifted people. We are children of our loving Father and day by day we are walking hand in hand with Him. But then we get depressed and say, God has abandoned me. You don't know what abandonment is. You don't know what emptiness is, believe me. But we can find God in a new and beautiful way by drawing into a deeper prayer life with Him. He has singled us out. He has called us. He wants to do a work in every one of our souls. He calls us to the Sacrament of Reconciliation. While we're walking this earth, the graces of God are sufficient to give us the ability, the desire to recyle our whole lives and become new creations. Now is the time, I say, my brothers and sisters, to change.

All I hear is the complaint, I don't know God. You don't know Him the way you want to know Him. But He knows you and He's with you. When I see you crawling and agonizing, then you can say, maybe, God has abandoned me. He never will.

Questioned about the case of a person who turns from God by deliberate mortal sin, Eileen replies that God is present pursuing that person by His grace.

8. Eileen and Archbishop Bevilacqua at the Philadelphia Rally, 1988

9. Eileen with Fr. Walter Ciszek, S.J., author of *God in Russia*, whose cause is being promoted

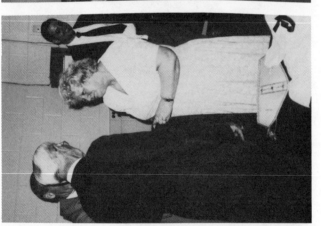

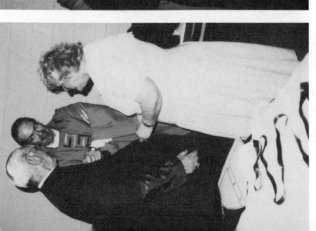

10. Eileen with Cardinal Krol, buttoning his robe, Msgr. Vincent Walsh in the background

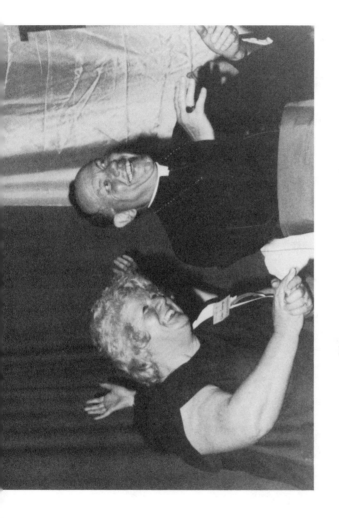

11. Eileen with Bishop Gelineau at the New Hampshire Charismatic Conference

12. Eileen with Archbishop Pearce, S.M. Archbishop Emeritus of the Fiji Islands

13. Eileen George

14. Father Hugh Nolan and priests at a retreat for the laity and religious at the Malvern Archdiocesan Retreat House

PART THREE

CHANNELS OF GRACE

Chapter Eight

The Holy Father

8.1 The Pope And Vatican II

If you stand firm on the doctrine and tradition of the Church, you will stand firm and defend our holy Father, John Paul II. He is truly a saint given to the Church. He is trying to bring the Church under the light of the Holy Spirit. He is not trying to make us into a medieval church as some say, "This is a medieval Pope, he is trying to put us back."

We ought to take another look at Vatican II, and see what is. making us tick! You will find out that a lot of things we are doing in our Church are not in Vatican II. Vatican II never told the women to take off their head dress. We did this. Why would Vatican II tell us to take off our head dress, and when we see the holy Father, we have to put on a veil? Is he greater than the Lord Jesus Christ? When I remarked to Cardinal Kim on how the Korean women, even children, wore a head dress in church, Cardinal Kim said: "Vatican II never told the women to take off the head dress—*you* did that!"

This is the hour the people are hungering after Jesus Christ. They are hungering after the Lord. The people have to know that their priests are deeply in love with Jesus. They will bring up questions about the Church, they'll bring up questions about the Pope, and they figure that that's when priests are going to waver. That's when priests have to say, No. Right is right, and wrong is wrong. And the people will know their priests belong totally to the Lord Jesus Christ. There is such a responsibility in this day and age for priests.

I'm not a theologian. All I know is that we should be obedient to the Holy Father. He's trying to keep us as Roman

Catholic people, he is trying to prevent the Church from dividing. We know the rules. We know how the Church is on abortion, on homosexuality, on divorce, on priests getting married or women being priests. The Pope is being defied openly. If the Holy Father says, No, it's no. If he says, Yes, I'll go along with it, because he's inspired to keep the Church in order.

See what is happening to our Church. The Pope is badly persecuted now, and a big persecution of the Church is coming. A handful will be left, and we had better make sure that we are among the handful.

8.2 The Churches Will Be Closed

I remember well the prophecy saying: The doors of the churches are going to be closed from the inside, not from the outside. The government is not going to board them up.

Priests must make sure they are Roman Catholic priests, living according to the rules. This is a dangerous time for our Church. Many divisions are coming among Catholics. This is the time each one of us, and myself included, have to look inside ourself, and say—not what is he all about, but what am I all about! It's a critical time for the Church. . . .

God is going to judge us, and especially priests, on how submissive we were to the holy Father. Those who are not submissive are scandalizing each other and our Church. We have to look within ourself. We may say, "Well, the Pope is not infallible, he makes a lot of mistakes." We're supposed to defend him.

That's what we should do with the holy Father. We know that he is a man, and he is capable of making mistakes, of course he is, but not when it comes to declaring the doctrine of the faith to the Church. It is up to us to defend him, not to tear him to pieces! As one Catholic to another, we have to hold him in a place of authority. If we are not under authority we are going to crumble; a house divided is going to fall. What is happening to us, to the Roman Catholic Church? We are a house divided and we are falling, we are going to fall unless we band together and stand close under the holy Father. Keep your eyes on the Lord! We are different!

We will not stand firm unless we spend time in personal prayer. Some people can only talk to God through a book, so that's the first stage of prayer. Then there comes a time when you put your books away, and talk to God from your heart. And in these quiet moments, you'll get the strength to defend the holy Father. You finally put the books away and in quiet moments say: Father, this is what I want to do, would you help me, Father? – then you are talking from your heart. And when you get deeper in prayer, then you get into contemplation, or wherever He wants to take you, but are we looking for this? Do we spend quiet moments with God? He's not way up there, He is right here. And sometimes we are too busy to have a heart to heart talk with Him. If we are too busy, we are not going to be faithful. If we hunger and thirst for the Lord, we are going to find strength.

8.3 Do Not Judge Priests

Do not judge priests. Love them. God says: Leave the judging to Me, you do the loving. Priests need to be encouraged and supported. Use your priests. Receive the sacraments from them – go to daily Mass, frequent the Sacrament of Reconciliation.

Chapter Nine

The Dignity Of The Priesthood:
The Mother Of A Priest

9.1 The Mother of a Priest

I sit upon my rocker and I look out into the garden at the flowers, the trees, the birds, and the butterflies. I look at all of God's creations: the sun, the sky, the clouds, and I rock, and I say, "O God, my Father, You have given me all this, and yet, you have given me an even greater gift, I am the mother of a priest, a priest of God Almighty."

My mind goes back to when my son was just a little boy. He used to come to me and sit at my knees and say, "Mother, talk to me about Jesus." I would tell him what my mother had taught me about Jesus. Another blessing, a grandmother who knew about Jesus! And he would listen with eager eyes and then run off to play like any other child. But as he grew, I noticed he was different. He played with other children, he did the things other boys did, but there was something unique about my son. O God in Heaven, could it be that you are calling him to be a priest? Can I bear the thought of losing him to my God? He will not have children to bring to my knees to call me Grandma. He will not give me a daughter, one that he holds as a wife. Am I willing to give this up? I needed a healing within me because I was feeling selfish.

9.2 I Wanted to Keep Him Close

We wanted him to be good and to love his God, but I didn't want to part with my son. We need priests, and this is good, but God forgive me, not my son. I wanted him to enjoy the better things of life, like being a husband, a father. And then I realized it was only my way of keeping him close to me, his mother. I watched him grow with anxiety, but in silence. I watched his reactions to worldly things and to holy things. I noticed he was becoming more gentle, more tender, more loving and mellow in his heavenly Father's love. I liked this, but I was afraid, "Dear God, is he going to become a priest?" I needed a grace so I could accept my son leaving me to become a priest. I prayed "God, help me. What is wrong with me?" It is surely a great thing to call my son to the priesthood, but I could not fully accept his leaving me.

Then the Lord spoke to my heart. It was I who also was being called to a vocation, the vocation of the mother of a priest. The Holy Spirit made me aware that this is a calling of its own. I had been called to be a wife and a mother, and now He was calling me to a new vocation. Could I accept this heavy role? How was I to face it? "O God in Heaven, what must I do?" Then it came time for my son to leave me. I felt resigned, and yet anxious, "O my son, my son, how long will you be away from me?"

9.3 Are You Calling My Son?

I held my head up high and I was thrilled when someone said, "Your son is going to be a priest." And I proudly proclaimed, "Yes, isn't it wonderful?" Yet, within me, "Dear God, is this right? Are you calling my son to the priesthood? Do You know what You are asking him to give up? Do You know what You are asking me to give up?" And as he went into the seminary, I became lonesome, but a surge of peace overtook my heart. My son, my very own son, is going to be a priest. He is going to call the Son of Almighty God, Jesus Christ, upon the altar. His hands will consecrate the host. This my son.

The days were long; I missed him. I sat alone and spent many hours in prayer asking God to help me understand the mystery of this great calling to the priesthood. I was fully aware, as the days slipped by, that God was easing me into my own vocation, the mother of a priest.

The day came when my son was to be ordained, and I went. My heart began to quicken. Does this mean it's the end of my son? He will no longer belong to me, he'll belong to the Church. What about his children whom I'll never see? I began to weep. Tears of sorrow, tears of emptiness. Yet, tears of joy. "Does my son fully understand what he has given up?" And then at once, like a bolt of lightning, I realized, he's not giving up, he's gaining. He has been called to be a holy priest of God Almighty. A high priest. A priest of the Holy of Holies. My son, my flesh and blood, my little boy, is going to call the Son of God from His Heavenly Court to come down upon the altar. He will distribute the Son of God to the brethren, to me, his mother. My son is going to hand me Jesus Christ, flesh and blood.

9.4 My Vocation as the Mother of a Priest

My son the priest. I realized the great vocation, the fulfillment that was ahead of me. Not only has God called my son, He has called me to a new vocation, the mother of a priest. "O, my God, will I have to be different? Will I have to be unique?" Now I began to worry about the responsibility that's upon my shoulders. And then I felt at peace. My son came to me afterward, and he kissed me, and he said, "Mother, thank you for being my mother. Thank you for being the mother you are, for this opened the door to my priesthood." And I began to understand. I don't have to change, God was pleased with the way I am. Even though I slip and fall, He was still pleased with me, and He called my flesh and blood to be a priest, a priest of the Almighty. The dignity of it! The majesty of it!

Now it was time to go to my son's first Mass. My heart was beating faster and faster. Does he know what to do? Will I know what to do? The altar boy lit the candles, and there came my son, clad in the robes of a high priest of God Almighty, to God's altar. He looked at me and he smiled, his sheepish, boyish little smile, but he was no longer a little boy, he was a priest of God Almighty. My heart swelled within my chest. "God my Father," I cried, "please help him. Enlighten his mind so he may not make a mistake, so he'll know what to do." He began the Mass and he knew what to do. My little boy look what you are doing! And my vocation as the mother of a priest came forth. He is no longer your little boy, he is a priest of the Almighty. He's your big boy. You are the mother of a priest.

He said Mass, and it was beautiful. In his homily, he thanked our heavenly Father for having blessed him with these two parents. That was me he was talking about! And my husband, his father! He thanked God and proclaimed that he was proud of us as parents! I could not stand any more, my heart was beating faster. I was so proud, so overwhelmed with holy joy. My son upon that pulpit, thanking God for giving me as his parent, my husband as a parent. My husband squeezed my hand, and we looked at each other.

And then it came time for holy communion. My knees felt like they were going to buckle as I went before my son as he said, "Take you and eat, this is the body of Jesus." And he put the body of Jesus upon my tongue. My son gave Jesus to me, his mother. What joy! What holiness! What dignity God has called me to! I wanted to shout to the world, "I am the mother of a priest! A priest of the Almighty. Look ye here all of you, this is my son! This is my little boy. A priest!" And then I realized, my vocation was being fulfilled, my new vocation, my new role, my new dignity, the mother of a priest.

9.5 A New and Beautiful Life

As I sit here and rock and rock and look out into the flower garden and reminisce, it seems like only yesterday, yet many, many years have passed. I have grown older, my son has grown older. He has found a new beautiful life as a priest. He visits me as often as he can, but in this vocation as the mother of a priest, I have learned not to be selfish. He is about his Father's business, a priest of the Almighty. I am the mother of a priest. I remember well when I became very sick and they thought that I would not live, it was my son, the priest, that prayed over me. The joy and the peace that filled my very soul when I heard my son's voice crying out to his heavenly Father, "O Father God, I ask You to touch and to heal my Mother." I heard my son pleading to the God that he served so well, for the healing of his mother. And even as weak and sick as I was, I could feel my heart swelling with joy and pride, listening to my son pleading with God the Father to heal his mother. My son, priest of Almighty God, what joy, what peace you brought into my heart! Our heavenly Father heard his prayers, and I was well.

As I sit in this rocking chair reminiscing, I think of the many times he came to the house and sat with me, like he used to sit as a little boy. And even now, at this moment, I thank Almighty God for having called my son to this unique calling of a priest. I thank our heavenly Father for having called me to this new vocation, the mother of a priest. I look at him with pride and spiritual joy. My son, may you always walk in God's love. May you always be a credit to your heavenly Father, for you are a priest of Almighty God. May you deal with the people in a loving, holy manner and may you reflect Jesus Christ to the brethren. May they look at you and say truly, "He is a priest."

9.6 The Dignity of the Mother of a Priest

Yes, I get lonely at times, but I know that my son, in giving his life to God the Father, and in dedicating his life to Jesus Christ the Son, has strengthened the faith of his mother. I know there is something beyond, because my son has given his life for it, and God has rewarded us both. He has rewarded our family. What a great honor it is to be the mother of a priest. I rock and I rock, where have all the years gone? It seems like only a blink of an eye that I held him on my lap, and on my knee, and he sat at my feet and we talked about this Jesus, and with a blink of an eye, he is grown up and is a priest. What a thought! I am the mother of a priest! My heart leaps for joy. "O Father in heaven, as I clasp my weary hands together, I bow my head in prayer, for I surely feel your presence. You have blessed me greatly because I have voluntarily given you my son. I know it wasn't easy to say *yes*, Father, but I have given him to you totally, and above all, lovingly. Father God, watch over this, my son, Your priest, my priest. With humble pride I say to You, Father, he is a good boy and may he always stay this way and be a credit to Your kingdom. May he save, through Your loving grace, many souls and bring them to his Father's throne. And may the humble prayers of his mother, sitting feebly in this chair, day after day, rise to you, heavenly Father, as incense, filled with love and understanding. I thank you for the great privilege You have given me.

My son you have brought to my heart such a dignity. I am proud to call you my son, my priest, and each night I thank God Almighty. "Father God, You know my words are true. I thank You for having found my son so special and unique in Your sight that You have called him to the priesthood. Father God, may I always set a good example to this, my son, for he has given me a new dignity in life. If all else shall fail me, I shall live on this, for this alone is enough my God, through your loving grace. This alone. I am the mother of a priest, a priest of God Almighty.

The tape here transcribed has been dedicated to the mother of Reverend Father Cyril A. LeBeau, my very dear friend, a mystical brother in Jesus Christ.

Chapter Ten

The Eucharist and Communion Songs

10.1 Ponce de Léon and the Fountain of Youth

Someone asked me, "Did Ponce de Léon ever find the fountain of youth?" He was looking for a fountain, which, if he drank from it, he would never die. Needless to say he never found this fountain.

But you and I have found the fountain of youth. We are going to be young forever; we can drink of that fountain. It's the Lord Jesus Christ in the Eucharist. "If you eat my Flesh and drink my Blood, you shall have life everlasting." Your body will die, but you will never die, you will live forever in the kingdom of Heaven.

But in order to understand this you need prayer time with the Lord so He can speak to your heart. Maybe we don't pray enough. It's not enough to say my faith is weak. That's a cop-out. You must practice your faith and make it strong. "I want to believe, Jesus." It's not enough to want to do something, you must put an effort into it. "I want to be a concert pianist." But if you just sit on your rump and don't practise, you'll never get there.

You see we have to put an effort into loving the Lord. The invitation is always there. The Son of God is inviting you to the banquet table. Maybe one or two come. How sad He must feel. "I send invitations out to all, only three answer that call. But that's o.k. I will still come through the words of the priest, and I will celebrate this great banquet, and I will give Myself to the three."

That's how important you are. He will not say, "The priest cannot bring me to the altar, there are only three here." O, He loves us. And what little love we give in return.

10.2 The Birthday Party

A child goes to the candy store as often as she can to satisfy her sweet tooth. She loves candy. She craves and desires its sweetness. And she is filled.

Jesus is the sweetness of all sweetnesses. We must have the same craving for the Eucharist as the child has for the candy. In all childlike trust we must go to the Eucharist and see how sweet He is, how He fills our very being. And how can we not give off the sweetness of the Lord?

Everyone loves a birthday party. No matter how old we are, we want the sweetness of the birthday cake, of the goodies and the secret gift. Well, be as a child and run to the party of all parties, where Jesus is the host, and you are indulging, not in a beautiful cake, but in all the graces that He has to give you.

The candles of faith will be the light, and you will be filled with the Holy Spirit. Your soul will spiritually clap its hands, and its eyes will beam and be radiant. For you will be celebrating the greatest of all parties, the party of Jesus Christ coming to your hearts, your very soul.

Every morning He comes, and taps on the door of your heart, inviting you to come to the Eucharist, and to let Him enkindle in your soul the candles of the Holy Spirit.

10.3 My Treasure

Many of us have treasures. It could be your mother's picture or your daddy's watch. It could be a lock of hair. You hold this treasure dear belonging to someone you love who has passed away. You keep this treasure in a secret place, perhaps in the china closet or under lock and key. Every once in awhile you take this treasure out and look at it. So insignificant to others, this treasure means so much to you. You begin to reminisce as you look at it, and sometimes, thinking how you miss this person, you shed tears. Sometimes you begin to laugh, thinking of all the happy times you had together, and you wish this person were present. Then, when you finish reminiscing, you put this little keepsake away in the secret place so it won't be lost, until you're ready to take this memory time back into your life.

Well, I have a treasure that I love more than anything in this world. I look at this treasure every day of my life. This treasure is Jesus Christ at daily Mass. I look at Him and sometimes when I receive Him I cry, thinking of His passion, all the abuse He took for love of me. I think of how many times I hurt Him and how many times I promised Him I'd be better, and then I let Him down again. I cry, asking Him to forgive me and to love me. Then at other times, I begin to laugh, thinking of all the crazy things we do together, and I think of the terrific sense of humor the Son of God has, just creating me. We have a great time together. But I don't put this treasure, the Lord Jesus Christ, back in a secret place and forget Him, I bring Him home in my heart, and I stay with Him all day, and I talk to Him, and I love Him. We discuss many things. This is the love I want each and every one of you to have for the Lord Jesus Christ.

Sometimes, when things get very difficult in your life, it's not that easy to turn towards Jesus with pure love. Instead, we turn towards Him with many questions. "Why me, Lord?" "What have I done to deserve this?" You've done nothing, it's just the path that we must walk: the way of the cross. It's not easy walking in the footsteps of Jesus Christ. Having such a great love for Jesus in the Eucharist, a love each of us should have, brings great sorrow and pain at times, when you see the abuse of the Eucharist, or the indifference of people.

I went to a service one day and I saw a person, very up in a church movement, chewing a big wad of gum. When she went to receive our blessed Lord, she took the wad of gum out of her mouth, received, and put it right back. It breaks my heart to see the abuse that He takes from us, maybe deliberately, hopefully not. We're lacking in love and we don't have enough faith. Most of the sins we commit against the Eucharist are sins of ignorance. It's very hard at times, and for me especially during Lent, to truly believe that the Lord Jesus Christ is there. But faith has to be exercised, faith has to be strengthened and nourished.

It's hard for us, as humans, to believe with all our heart that the Lord Jesus Christ is really in the tabernacle. What must we do? We must say, "Jesus, I know You're there. You instituted the Eucharist at the Last Supper. Increase my faith. Make me strong." And He will.

10.4 Sensitivity

To be so in love with Jesus, our Eucharistic King, can give a person much pain. I preach in the United States and outside it, and wherever I go I see irreverences every day. A priest said to me, "I can't believe you are so sensitive about the Eucharist." And all I could say was, "My God, you're a priest." He said this because something happened at the altar, and I began to cry. My heart was broken. But this sensitivity should be in each and every one of us and it doesn't come over night. It doesn't come through a magic wand. It comes from practising your faith every day of your life.

When I hunger for Him so much, it tells Him how much I love Him. That's what I want for you. I don't care if you move mountains. I don't care if you heal the people. I don't care if you speak many languages through the Spirit. I don't care if you fall down in the Spirit. I want you to be excited about coming and receiving Him. I want you, if you do wake up at night, not to grumble, "O Lord, let me sleep." It's o.k. to say that, but let your heart beat fast because you're going to Mass that morning. I want you to be so in love with Jesus, that your whole world will change. I want you to radiate love for your Eucharistic King.

Jesus knew everything He was going to go through. The agony in the garden. The crowning with thorns. The scourging. The scourging wasn't just the beating with a strap, the scourge had metal claws, so when it struck the Lord, it dug into His skin and tore His flesh. Jesus anticipated all this, but the love was there to go through it. In spite of what He knew was going to happen, He gave you His body and His blood, the Eucharist. We take it so lightly, my brothers and sisters. We come up out of habit, like robots. This is the embrace of the Lord Jesus Christ! Feeling His kiss upon your lips and His blood going through your veins, you become whole. We're Christians. Being followers of the Lord Jesus Christ doesn't just mean going to Mass on Sunday. It means falling in love with Him.

How can you follow someone, or say you're following someone, you don't love? I certainly wouldn't follow somebody I didn't love. You have to love Jesus to follow Him. And when you follow Him, your whole life changes. You're never alone. Maybe it takes a dark night of the soul to open you up to all the blessings of being a Christian. Maybe it takes something like this to make you feel the pain of loss. But we have Him here all the time. Don't pass Him by. Don't wait until your deathbed to cry out, "Lord, save me!" You may not have the grace to do it then. I want each of you to be so in love with our Eucharistic King, that if someone came and said, "If you don't deny Him, I will kill you," you'd say, "Kill me." Can you say that? I often wonder. And yet, we proclaim to the world, we're Roman Catholic Christians, we're Christians.

We don't know what we're all about. We don't know what Jesus is all about. We look up at the crucifix and we're not moved. We hear about the passion during Lent, but we're not touched.

I said that Jesus anticipated all the pain of the passion. When I was a little kid, my Mother never hit me. She'd threaten, "Wait until Daddy comes home." When my father came home, he'd do the job. Daddy had a big, thick razor strap. Sometimes I'd hide it on him. Most of the time he wouldn't want to hit me. He'd say to my Mother, "O Maisey, how bad could it be?" My Mother would say, "Terrible." So I would go up to my room and he'd come up with the razor strap, and we'd be looking down at my Mother. She'd be over the old black stove, and she'd yell up through the grating, "Lou, you make sure you give it to her!" And he'd say, "When I hit the wall, you yell." So he'd hit the wall and I'd yell, "No, Daddy. Help. Help. No Daddy!" And we'd look down at my Mother. She'd say, "That's enough, Lou, that's enough! I didn't tell you to kill her!" But that wasn't always the case. Sometimes I'd get it across you-know-where. And rightfully so. But the point is, when I did something naughty, I anticipated that I might get that strap. It was agony all day long. Christ anticipated His beatings, His thorns. What blows my mind when I think of this is the love He held for us, to give us the Eucharist.

10.5 His Love For Us Is Hard To Grasp

You'd say, "Lord, haven't you got enough to think about? Why are you doing this for us?" "Because I love you so much." But how many of us go to Mass and communion as often as we can, even during the holy, joyful season of Lent. It seems as though we're just too busy. But that's how you fall in love with Him. I know it's hard to grasp, and I don't want you going to Mass out of habit. "Who's going to see me?" But I want you to say as you're going, "It's hard for me to grasp, Jesus. I'm only human. I have to see, feel and touch. Jesus, stimulate in my heart a burning love for You."

I want you to love Jesus with your heart, your mind, your body, and your soul. To fall madly in love with Jesus. You'll never feel alone again, no matter what the trial is, you can get through that trial. But do we give Him a chance to take part in our lives?

I thought the painter of the picture of Christ knocking at the door was negligent, he didn't finish the painting, he didn't put a door knob in the picture. Jesus is outside knocking at your heart. He won't enter. The doorknob is on the inside, you have to open the door to let Him in. He won't force you to love Him in the Eucharist. It breaks my heart that we come week after week, and we don't even look towards Him in the tabernacle and say, "I love You, Lord." Oh, He's so happy, He's delighted that you're here. But did you look towards that tabernacle and pour out your love for Him? "Jesus, I want to love You. Help me." If the Holy Father was sitting there, you'd all be looking at Him.

10.6 On Being A Sanctuary Lamp

In the chapel of Anna Maria College, I was telling the sanctuary lamp, "I'm jealous of you, sanctuary lamp. You can stay by the tabernacle all day and be close to the Lord, but I have to go on my merry way. Yes, I'm jealous of you. I wish I were a sanctuary lamp." Then the Father spoke to my heart and said, "Eileen, you can be the living sanctuary lamp that walks out amongst My people, and gives new light to the world saying, 'God lives here within me.' " I think of that often. Each one of us can be the living sanctuary lamp. God lives in our hearts and dwells in us. Well if He does, be radiant in His love, be joyful in His love. You are the human torches that spread the word of Christ.

10.7 Becoming a New Creation

When we receive Him we feel His kiss upon our lips and the warmth of His very being within our soul. What joy and what peace! If we don't have that joy and peace but go out and get in the same old rut, we're lacking something. We're going to renew ourselves so that we can truly say, "I'm a new creation by grace and acceptance of grace. I am rising from my old, drab human nature, with Christ, to a new spiritual being, because it's no longer I who lives, but Christ Who dwells within me." This is what it means to love Jesus, to take off the old man, or woman, and put on Christ. Everybody will find a change in you, and they'll say, "He, or she, is going through a trial, but look how well they carry their cross."

I had a call from a Jewish person. He said to me, "Eileen, God deals with you in a very special way. I know what I should be doing, but I'm going to leave it all up to God. I'm not going to interfere with the plan He has for you." Maybe someday I'll be able to tell you what this is all about. He's a very kosher Jew. He has all the right in the world to interfere with things that are happening to me, but he said, "I know God is working with you. I'm not going to interfere with His plan." That blew me away.

This man is coming closer to Christ. Before he hung up the phone, he said, "Eileen, did you receive your Jesus today?"

"Yes, but He's also your Jesus."

"Do you think I have accepted Him in my heart yet?"

"Yes, I know you have. The way you speak about the Father, and the way you call him Jesus. There's a mellowness in your tone."

"Do you think that someday I will receive this Jesus?" He was fishing, but not making a commitment to becoming a Christian.

"I know without a doubt the day that I leave here will be the day of your conversion." He almost died.

He said, "Eileen, I want you to stay here forever. That's why I'm not interfering with you." And I could tell he was crying.

He said, "I'm going to stand on this word, because I know it's from Him." But imagine that. He feels the love in my heart for my Jesus. That same love I want each one of you to feel. Just concentrate on loving your Eucharistic King.

10.8 His Presence

Don't worry about big penances and big sacrifices and giving up all your desserts. That's good. But the most important thing is to concentrate on His presence in the tabernacle and the love Jesus Christ has for you, and the love you want to give Him. Say, "Lord, open my heart spiritually. Open my heart and pour all Your love in. I want to be a new creation by grace." All you have to do is to fall deeper in love with Him. So if you do see some irreverence, you'll feel that pang in your heart. You can't feel the pang, if you don't have this love.

At many places I go to preach, they want to put our blessed Lord in the monstrance while I'm preaching. And I say, "No, I won't let you do this, I won't preach." And it can very well be high authority. They'll say, "Why?" I say, "I will not stand on the podium and have my back to the Lord Jesus Christ, when He's looking over His people. I will not have the people looking at me and listening to me and ignoring the Lord Jesus Christ." That's being sensitive. If you really believed, you wouldn't do these things. And don't think I don't get whiplashes for this. "I'm this," and "I'm that," and "It's o.k." No, not in my heart. When I'm on the podium, you're listening to me. When Jesus is in the monstrance, all attention should be given to the Lord Jesus Christ. He's not to take a second place to Eileen, God forbid. This is sensitivity to the Eucharist.

When you come into church, genuflect or make a profound bow, and say, "O Jesus, it's good to be here." Talk to Him; don't ignore Him. I know we don't do it willfully. Pour out your heart to Him. There's nothing that we have, illness, trials or tribulations, that He can't remedy. So pour out your love to Him. Is it so difficult to love Him? Why? A cat gets more love than the Lord Jesus Christ. My dogs get more love than the Lord Jesus Christ, and it breaks my heart. The clothes we wear probably get more attention than the Lord Jesus Christ. What are we all about? Are we all about rubies and diamonds and coats and cars and furniture, or are we all about Jesus? Let's look within ourselves. He loves us so much. Even if we ignore Him, He pursues us by grace. What a lover. I tell you one thing, you've never been kissed, until you've been kissed by the Lord. You've never been loved until you've been loved by the Lord. Now is the hour. Fall in love with Jesus. Praise the Lord Jesus Christ.

10.9 What Will People Remember Me For?

Many times I wonder, if I should die, what will people remember me for? Will it be that I always smiled? The time I smile the most, my husband knows something's bugging me. He'll say, "O.K., what's the matter, Hon? Come and tell Dad." Will they remember me for my sense of humor? Will they remember me for my healings?

When I wake up at night, I check the clock and I say, "O Jesus, in a few hours I'll be receiving You." My heart begins to beat so fast with love and holy expectation to receive Jesus in the Eucharist.

And then I said, "I hope they will remember me for my great love for the Lord Jesus Christ in the Eucharist."

10.10 COMMUNION SONGS AND POEMS

These songs were given to Eileen in tongues at her communions. By the gift of interpretation she grasped their meaning in English.

In the Shadow of My Love

In the shadow of My love,
Eileen, you will find Me.
In the shadow of My love,
You will know that I am there.

I'll hold you close,
I'll hold you tight.
I'll love you, Child,
With all My might.

You will be a victim of
The Father's delight.

In the shadow of My cross,
I'll love you, Eileen
In the shadow of My cross,
I'll hold you.

Grown to an Adult Size

Now you've grown to an adult size,
Nothing but love in both our eyes.
The Father has wed you,
He stands by your side
To love you,
To protect you,
To draw you close.

The Kingdom Revealed

The peace of the kingdom engulfs me,
And no man can take this from me.

It is mine and mine alone to have.
It's a gift from my Father,
A spiritual bouquet from one who loves me.

I will hold this sinless
And precious within my soul,

Only when I am gone,
And free from this world of travail,
To be with my Father,
Will the world know that the kingdom
Has been revealed to this little one.

Confine Me.

I pass through thee, my love,
As a quiet gentle breeze.
And yet I do not go through thee.

You hold me captive within Thee.
I do not want to be free.
O my Love, hold me.
Hold me captive within Thee.

If you let me pass through Thee,
I may run on and on,
Through the meadows
And over the mountain tops.
And I will lose my way,
My way back to Thee.
No my Love, keep me here.

If sometimes I get stronger
And tug on
The strings of Thy heart
Please continue to confine me.
I love Thee, I love Thee.

Trust in Me, the Shepherd.

Eileen, I am your Shepherd
And you are the sheep,
And you are very special to Me.

I will find you a place to sleep,
A home,
And waters of grace to drink.

I will watch over you
And coddle you,
Caress and love you.

And no harm shall befall you.
I will take care
Of all your needs.

You know how a Shepherd
Follows His sheep.
Trust in Me, the Shepherd.

All Because I Love You.

I take you to our secret place.
I hold your hand, I kiss your cheeks,
You feel My embrace.

I hold you in My arms, My dear,
I draw you close,
I touch your hair,

I kiss your lips.
I feel your warmth,
All because I love you.

The rains may come
The snow may fall
I'll hold you close.
You'll stand so tall
Above the world,
Above the people,
All because I love you.

I cut you free
From all the world
Because I love you.

My lips press against yours,
I feel your heart, we're one.

No man can free us
Or pull us apart.
All because I love you.

Our hearts entwine,
Our lips are warm
Pulses racing
There is but one form
All because I love you.

Look upon us
Heavenly court
And rejoice,
For I am with my lover.

Let there not be envy,
Nor let jealousy arise,

But warmth, admiration,
All because I love you.

With such tenderness
You call my name.

Yes, all because
I love you.

I cannot wait another day.
I need you here forever.
All because I love you.

I Will Remember

When I awake,
And I seem to be alone,
I call His name,
It rings out,
But no answer returns.
And I look to the right,
And I look to the left,
And I see Him not,
And fear grips my heart,
Loneliness falls upon my soul.

My memories will reach out,
And say, He loves me,
Trust in Him.

And I run to every secret place,
And find it empty.
He's not here,
And fear grips my heart again.
I will remember the words
Eileen, I love you,
Trust Me.

I will run to the meadows,
And lay in our secret place.
And ask the flowers,
Have you seen Him?
And they will not respond,
Nor answer.
And fear will grip my heart,
And emptiness my soul
And I will remember His words:
Eileen, I love you,
Trust me.

Into Your Father's Side

The Peace of your God
Will overshadow you,
And no matter how you are rebuffed
By the evil of men,
Or by Capi,
You will not be torn down.
You will find peace and truth.

As gently
As a feather falls
From a bird,
You will fall
Deeper into
Your Father's side.

Go On

*Poem given in tongues during the morning Friday, Dec. 30, 1988.
Eileen had slipped on a wet floor and hurt her wrist and bruised her
knees. She was hurting badly. She had had numerous afflictions,
fatigue, continual illnesses of one kind or another, and now
discouragement set in.*

As at the moment I felt, O, gee, I can't go on, something like a breeze whisked through the house. It said, You can't rest, you've got to go on and on; never mind your humanness. The sun was pouring in from the window over the counter top, and it seemed to warm me so, encouraging me to go on. Then I heard this song:

> At times my mountain
> Seems so high to climb,
> My strength so very weak.
> My body wants to stop
> And permanently rest.
>
> But my soul pushes me on,
> To climb, step by step,
> The mountain which is so steep.
>
> Through the rustle of the trees
> I hear the wind call my name:
> Climb higher, climb higher, dear,
> Climb higher.
>
> I feel His kiss upon my cheek
> Encouraging me to go on.
> And the sun shines upon me
> To warm the chill, the humidity
> Channeled through my bones.
>
> The call of the wind
> Keeps ringing in my ears:
> Climb higher, Child, keep climbing.

Chapter Eleven

The Healing Sacrament

11.1 The Wounded Deer

There was a tiny tame deer running around Greenwood Park with an arrow in its temple. Someone had shot this deer. People were trying to capture it to pull out the arrow and to treat the wound. The Father said, That's the way my children are when they need confession. They have a poisoned arrow within their soul. The only doctor who can pull it out is the priest, and the ointment is the penance and to be reconciled with God with the purpose of not repeating this sin.

11.2 The Response of the Waltham Retreatants (1988)

I was amazed at the Waltham retreatants. They were so filled, they were on fire with the love of God. The second day there was no holding them back. They were hungering and thirsting after the Lord. They wouldn't care if we stayed in chapel ten hours as long as they were with the Lord.

The first night I begged them to begin their retreat by the Sacrament of Reconciliation, to get back into the loving arms of the Father. Every one in that place went to confession, and there were over one hundred seventy people. Because they knew the value of confession. And the next day they were set on fire with the love of God.

They confessed their sins, they opened the spiritual doors of their hearts, and God's graces and blessings entered in and watered the spiritual garden of their souls, and then new taste buds sprang forth. Instead of hungering and thirsting for the things of the world, they were hungering and thirsting and panting after God. It was wonderful. They came from every walk of life.

You see, that's what I want from you, to hunger and thirst, to actually pant, after God. But we must follow the proper channels. Go to the Sacrament of Reconciliation, get reconciled with your God, and once you are reconciled with your God, you can hear His loving call, because He is the Beloved, "Come, My love, My dove, My beautiful one, accept My invitation, come and dine with Me at the banquet table of daily Mass!"

11.3 The Sacrament of Reconciliation

This is the way Eileen begins her retreats: You know a retreat is exactly what it says. We're retreating from the world and getting back into the loving arms of our Father. I want you to have time to think about the message which the Father has given you through Eileen, to dwell on it, and apply it to your own lives.

I like to begin with the Sacrament of Reconciliation; we all need this Sacrament. It opens the spiritual doors of the soul. Then God's graces will flood your soul, and then new flowers and new taste buds will spring forth, not for the world but for the things of God. God wants to do a work in your soul. He wants to love you. You have to get rid of the turmoil of faults and sin, so that God can do the wonderful work He intends to do. He wants you to hear His voice. In order to hear His voice, you have to be silent. In order to be silent the soul has to be quieted through the Sacrament of Reconciliation.

PART FOUR

KOREA AND AMERICA

Chapter Twelve

Eileen in Korea – 1986

By Brother DePorres Stilp, M.M.

12.1 The Massive Healing Rally

"I am making another covenant with my people, because you come here to praise, worship, and give glory to your God."

May 16th, 1986, Buddha's 2530th birthday, provided a holiday in Korea, enabling some twelve thousand Catholics and others from Seoul and nearby cities, to hear the teachings of, and receive the healing ministry of, Mrs. Eileen George, the year's invited speaker to Korea. She is being sponsored by the National Korean Catholic Charismatic Renewal Service Committee.

The setting for the massive healing rally was the open air grounds of the seminary of Seoul which was graced with a perfect day of clear blue sky. On this occasion, her Father provided a heavenly touch for the gathering by having a unique rainbow appear in the sky during the offertory of the Mass, which began at 11:00 A.M. This rainbow remained about twenty minutes and was seen and marvelled at by all. It was accepted as a supernatural sign. Eileen remarked that it was not opposite the sun, the normal place for a rainbow, but directly under the sun. Also it was not curved, but straight and horizontal. The Father spoke in prophecy to the people through Eileen, saying that it was a sign of a new covenant of peace He was making with His dear Korean people, to express His great pleasure at their steadfast acceptance of the Charismatic Renewal.

The healing service in the afternoon was the first experience of its kind for Catholics in Korea. Mrs. George's extraordinary gift of receiving the Lord's word of knowledge in such a direct, precise, and singular way electrified the large crowd of believers beyond their expectations. Eileen called out more than fifty spiritual and physical healings during the hour-long service. When they were singled out, people responded by standing and claiming their healings, and acknowledging that it was they she was referring to either by dress, sex, age, name, sickness or by events, such as marriages being healed.

Some of the physical healings included opening of ears, healing of eyes, rheumatoid arthritis and osteoarthritis, insomnia, lumps on women's breasts, cancer, bronchitis, women's disorders, flow of blood, blood disorders, and perhaps most touching of all, the healing of a number of young children and polio victims. A twelve year old child with cerebral palsy who had never walked before began to walk [see picture].

There were also spiritual healings of personal relationships, of families, of parents with their children, return to the sacraments, gifts of faith, etc. Eileen lovingly assured the people that all who attended would be healed and touched in some special way by the Father's love and mercy. This was received with a resounding round of applause.

12.2 Missionary Journey in Korea

Pentecost Sunday May 18, Eileen George, Claire Collins (Eileen's companion), Andrew Chong, National Charismatic Renewal Office Director, and Brother DePorres, M.M., bordered the 9:00 A.M. express train at the Seoul station for Taegu, the southern capital city of the Kyaong Sam Pok province. It was a three and a half hour ride, and to our surprise Eileen revealed that it was her first train journey. The small mission band celebrated Pentecost morning by watching the beautiful rolling lands of the Korean landscape. As it was high spring they saw rows and rows of farmers and volunteers hard at work planting the new rice seedlings, one by one, in endless water field rice patties, a job all pitch in to do.

These ten days of circuit will include the six cities of Taegu, with a population of two million, Pusan, three million, Masan 500,000, Maupu 300,000, KwangJu one million, and ChongJu 400,000. All will be one day events either being combined afternoon and evening events, or just a longer afternoon event. It will give many people the opportunity to receive the good news from an international speaker for the first time.

At Taegu the band was joined by Sister Gemma Paik, a Benedictine sister who traveled with them as translator for the next ten days. The event was held in a Catholic women's college auditorium. More than three thousand squeezed in, overflowing onto the stage. Almost every place Eileen went it proved almost impossible for all to get into the site selected.

At Pusan, May 21, a famous southern port city, the event was hosted at a local girls' high school auditorium, with an overflowing crowd of three thousand. Bishop Gabriel Lee, Bishop of Pusan celebrated Mass. He asked Eileen if she would kindly come and pray with one of his retired priests, Father Majea Park, aged 75, who had not said Mass for the past ten years. He had suffered from migraine from seminary days. Coupled with this were the changes in the Church after Vatican II, so that he lay down on his bed with little desire to get up again. She promised the Bishop she would. Before leaving Pusan on the morning of the 22nd, she went to meet this gentle priest. She listened to his story and was happy to hear that it was he himself who had enlisted the Bishop's intervention. She prayed for him and encouraged him to begin celebrating Mass again, saying with prophetic words that his healing would progress with each daily Mass he said.

Brother DePorres who was translating then suggested to Father that even today he might like to offer Mass for Eileen, since her little group had not had Mass this day, as all the Pusan diocesan priests were on their annual retreat.

To everyone's surprise, he agreed, and immediately asked the parish sister to arrange a table in his sitting room as the altar. He rose from his sick bed, and offered a Latin Mass for all. The prayer had begun to take effect! Later Eileen confessed that this was the highlight of her trip to Korea. If this alone had happened in her stay, she would have been completely satisfied.

12.3 Completing the Journey

Friday May 23, the local leader at Masan arranged to have the healing service in the Catholic girls' high school auditorium. Some three thousand three hundred gathered for the afternoon service, the number far exceeding the thousand who had been expected. This was the first time such a charismatic event had been held in this small diocese.

On Saturday morning May 24, began the long trek by car over some of the most mountainous and isolated areas of the Korean peninsula. Even with the new expressway, it took almost six hours. The natural beauty of the mountains was enjoyed by our visitors.

Lopo, the next destination, is on the Yellow Sea, the western side of the peninsula. It is a harbor city of some 300,000 inhabitants. Off the shore are more than four hundred islands, many of them inhabited. The Lopo priests serve these islands as part of their three parishes as mission stations. The Columban sisters of Ireland and the United States have been operating a semi-charity hospital here for some thirty years, and it was with them that Eileen and her party stayed. It proved providential as Eileen was tired and suffering from a deep chest cold picked up at the May 16th rally in Seoul. The Columban sisters welcomed her with warm hospitality, and Sister David, a medical doctor, treated her cold. Unexpectedly she had a violent reaction to the penicillin, and suffered with chills and fever during the night. She recovered sufficiently to give the afternoon teaching and healing service on Saturday afternoon May 25th to more than two thousand people, many of them from the scattered islands. The same evening the small band continued on to KwongJu, the fifth city on the six city tour.

The hosts for Eileen were the Columban Fathers, at their center house in KwongJu. The southwestern mission was originally developed by the Columbans in the late 1930s, when it was given them upon their arrival to work in Korea. It was headed for many years by American Columban missioner and prelate, Archbishop Harold Henry from Minnesota. In those early years, when more than thirty Columban missioners were stationed in this area, the center house was established for them.

12.4 St. Andrew Kim

This was the setting for a miracle of deep spiritual meaning for Koreans. At the center house Father Frank Royer, Columban from Chicago, placed her in the guest-room next to the chapel. She retired early after arrival to rest and recover her strength for the two remaining events of the trip, KwongJu the next morning and ChongJu the day following. At 2:30 A.M., in the deepest part, of the night, she heard someone call her name. She turned to see who it was, and was startled to see a Korean man standing in the corner of her room. He was surrounded by an aurora of light which made him visible. She asked in English who he was. He replied in Korean, but she understood him, although she knows no Korean. He said his Christian name is Andrew. He had come to thank her for coming from her far-off country to visit and minister to his "children." She was perplexed by these words, as she knew that only God had spiritual children here in Korea. He assured her again that he was pleased that she had come and he said that through her ministry in Korea many would be blessed with the light of faith and with a greater knowledge of God.

He was handsome with fine round features, and a small mustache and beard. He was about twenty-five years of age, and wore a long white robe like an alb, and around his neck a white stole, by which she understood that he was a priest. This stole was permeated by light. The strangest part of his dress was a wide brim hat with a stove pipe-like cone in the middle. She described it as like wire-screening material, that one could see through. He came over to her – actually floated as he was raised about five inches above the floor – and laid his hands on her head. She felt his hands on her head.

After this, he backed away a few paces without turning and disappeared into the darkness of the night. In the morning she confided this happening to Brother DePorres who helped to identify this heavenly visitor. He told her the story of St. Andrew Kim, a young Korean destined to become the first Korean priest at the age of twenty-four. She was surprised by this revelation, and said that he would return again.

12.5 Ordination of Andrew Kim

During the first two hundred years or more of the beginnings of Catholicism in Korea, foreigners were not allowed to enter the country. The Paris Foreign Missionary Society was assigned to care for Korea, and made many attempts to do so. Father Peter Maubant entered the country in 1836, one of three French missionaries to succeed in doing so. They ministered to the five thousand hidden and scattered Catholics as best they could. Father Maubant realized that the key to the successful future of the Korean mission was a native clergy, for foreigners could not go undetected among the Koreans, and Koreans were forbidden to associate with foreigners under penalty of death. So the same year he sent three promising youths to Macao, spiriting them out of Korea down through China to their seminary there.

In 1845 the newly appointed Bishop to Korea, French missioner Msgr. Jean-Joseph Ferreol took Deacon Andrew with him to help him get into Korea through the northern border on the Yellow River. Andrew entered and reported back to the Bishop, who decided to ordain him ahead of his time of studies so that he could be of immediate service to the priestless Korean Catholics, the three French missioners having been killed in the persecution of 1839.

Andrew was ordained on August 17, 1845 and eventually reentered his native land, commissioned by his Bishop to send him a report on the state of the Church in Korea and on the best way of bringing newly arriving French missionaries into the country.

In a small port on the Yellow Sea, while negotiating with kindly sailors to send his report to his Bishop, who was awaiting it in China, Andrew was captured. He was imprisoned in August 1846, only one year after his ordination, exposed not only as a dreaded Catholic, but also as a priest, one who associated with foreigners. He was sentenced to death and was beheaded on September 16, 1846 at the age of twenty-five. His letters from his prison cell remind one of Paul's epistles from his prison.

It was this young priest who appeared to Eileen on the morning of May 27 in KwongJu. She was not prepared to tell this story to anyone, but at the morning session at the KwongJu Cathedral, the Holy Spirit prompted her to reveal this heavenly visitor to the large gathering of Koreans. When they heard this story, they were electrified and delighted. It was the first time that anyone had had such an encounter with the popular priest saint, and they were thrilled. And this happened to a non-Korean!

12.6 ChongJu

After KwongJu, the small band of travellers arrived at ChongJu the last city on their circuit. This was the first time in the ten year history of the Charismatic Renewal that this provincial capital city had had an international speaker. And as the adage goes of "saving the best for last," this turned out to be the most marvelous event of all nine provincial cities visited.

The local leaders, expecting a crowd of three or four thousand, were overwhelmed when over ten thousand packed the indoor stadium of the city. Brother DePorres, a veteran of these yearly events, was "floored" by this almost miraculous turnout – almost as large as the national rally held on May 16th at Seoul. It was super in all ways: in the preparations made by the committee, the beautiful Korean dresses of the ladies who acted as guides, and the great expectation and joy in the people. Eileen was especially brimming on this day for she revealed to the crowd that St. Andrew had healed her of her heavy cold and weakness when he laid his hands on her head the day before.

The only flaw in the program, but perhaps a hidden blessing, occurred at the last event of the day, Mass at 4:30. It was abruptly cancelled when tear gas used by the riot police in their clash with demonstrating college students next door to the stadium wafted into the overcrowded stadium. Bishop Michael Park of ChongJu, who was to celebrate the Mass, thought it best for all to leave immediately.

This was the largest Catholic gathering in the history of the ChongJu diocese! On the long ride back to Seoul on the following day, May 28th, the journey was broken up with a visit to "Flower Village," a haven in the hinterland of Korea for five hundred fifty men and women who are rejected by society. They are being cared for by a nationally known charismatic Korean priest, Rev. John Ho, who has dedicated his priesthood to helping the poor. Besides the inmates, five hundred friends of Father John's work gathered for the short teaching and the healing service.

12.7 Eileen Returns Home

The last event of Eileen's ministry in Korea was a two day retreat in Seoul for over four hundred Korean sisters May 29–30. During this time a great love flowed between the speaker and the retreatants. At the conclusion Eileen embraced each sister as a farewell gesture, an act which took an hour and a half!

Eileen George ministered to more than 46,000 people during her month's stay in Korea. She met many of the American and European missionaries. She was surprised to encounter— some at the Maryknoll Center where she stayed in Seoul—a number from her New England area, Most Rev. William J. McNaughton, Bishop of Inchon diocese, native of Lawrence, Mass., and Bro. Justin Joyce, M.M. of Fitchburg, Mass. Also Father Fernand Taquet, M.M. and Father MacInnis, M.M. of Maine; Father Carl Costa, M.M. and Sister Marie Crawley, Maryknoll sister, from Boston. The latter is also a friend of Claire Collins. And finally Sister Anne Dundin, Franciscan Missionary from

Rhode Island, stationed in Pusan. Mention has also been made of the Columban sisters and fathers.

June 3rd Eileen left Korea on her flight home, with many memories of this fabulous month. So many tender moments of weeping and gloriously happy people receiving the healing touch of "Daddy God," the endless steps taken up or down stages, or behind stages, to avoid the adoring crowds who wanted to touch and reach out to her.

Eileen told them at each gathering, that they had stolen her heart as no others had done. In turn they have extracted a promise from her that she will return in 1989 if Father God allows her that much more time. She has been an evangelizer par excellence for her "Daddy God," and all have enjoyed her uplifting, inspiring, yet solid theology! She has taught them to use every moment of every day as offerings to God for souls, explaining that she offers every dish that she wipes, every room that she cleans for the salvation of souls. Everything in life that is common can be uncommon or heavenly common. She explained the seven levels or plateaus of heaven, and urged all to strive for the Seventh Heaven, assuring them that not only the extraordinary saints arrive there, but that anyone can strive for and reach the Seventh Heaven by the Father's grace. Heaven is for everybody who wants it. She likens Father God to a grandfather. When she gets mad at her three year old grandchild for breaking dishes or messing up the house, her grandchild runs to her grandfather, climbs onto his lap, gives him a hug and kiss, says she is sorry, grandpa, and he embraces her and says that's o.k.—and gives her the house! So too the Father is very willing and ready to welcome us with open arms, to forgive us, and to bring us to Himself.

Eileen we welcome you back!

12.8 Korea's Message To U.S.A. (Editor's Note)

Eileen found in the Korean Church some of the things she has been recommending to her American people. She found a lively faith in, and devotion to, Jesus in the Eucharist on the part of both people and priests, and a deep respect on the part of the people for their priests.

The people never tired of teaching. During the healing services, they would claim their healings, standing up and waving their arms above their heads, and sometimes clapping their hands. The people turned out in large numbers for services from one thousand to twelve thousand.

Now Eileen is telling priests and people in this country to wake up! Wake up to the faith, to the life of personal holiness, become loving people! That is the message she has brought back from Korea.

(This story appeared in the Worcester Catholic Free Press. At the time, Brother De Porres Stilp, M.M., was the liaison for the National Korean Catholic Charismatic Renewal Service Committee).

15. Eileen and Claire Collins being welcomed to Korea by Stephen Cardinal Kim in 1986. Present are Andrew Chong and Brother DePorres Stilp, M.M. (hidden behind Eileen).

16. Eileen and more than 400 sisters at her retreat in Seoul

17. Eileen embracing the sisters at the end of her retreat

18. Paralyzed child who had never walked, healed at Eileen's service in Korea in 1986, ascends the podium to embrace Eileen.

Chapter Thirteen

Korea Revisited – 1989

By Fr. James Caldarella

13.1 Eileen's Enthusiastic Reception

Eileen George returned Tuesday May 30th from a strenuous teaching and healing tour of South Korea, which began April 30th. I arrived in Seoul on May 10 to join her party for two weeks during her journey to nine dioceses. She had already given a retreat to thirty-three priests, directed teaching and healing services in three neighboring dioceses, conducted a "Night of Grace" at the Seoul Cathedral in the presence of Stephen Cardinal Kim, and given a retreat to twenty-three hundred national lay leaders.

Before we left Seoul, Mrs. George gave a teaching and healing service to thirty thousand people in the Olympic Gymnastic Stadium in the presence of the Apostolic Delegate and two Bishops. Throughout the country thousands gathered and sat for hours eager to hear her words, just as many have assembled in different parts of the United States to receive her teaching with enthusiasm. Before leaving Korea, she had ministered to eighty-four thousand people.

The expectant faith of the Koreans was rewarded by teachings from the Father, powerful prophecies, and miraculous healings confirming the words Eileen spoke. Her hearers were brought closer to Jesus and to His Father, as she urged them not to seek the gifts of God but the Giver of the gifts, and to welcome the Holy Spirit, the Third Person of the Trinity, into their hearts. She encouraged all to be united to the bride of the Holy Spirit, the Blessed Mother.

13.2 The Korean Church

Profoundly moving was the reverence of the Korean people for their priests, the Eucharist, and the Church. The crowds were a sea of white as women covered their heads for the celebration of Mass. Eucharistic ministers washed their hands before taking the ciboria to distribute communion, and waited in the front aisles for the priests to bring the ciboria to them from the sanctuary.

The Korean culture gives preeminence to men in church and civil affairs. Eileen quickly overcame this handicap. Brother DePorres Stilp, M.M. told how the Korean people had fallen in love with Eileen – and she with them.

The Korean Church, a Church of martyrs, is young, fervent, and expanding rapidly. In each diocese the rapid growth of the Church was mentioned. Many churches have five hundred converts a year. People stop Catholics on the street saying, "You are so happy, I want what you have." The seminaries are filled. And yet often in the first year after ordination the priest becomes a pastor.

One of the moving experiences occurred at Cheju Island. Bishop Paul Kim had expressed his eagerness to have Eileen come to his diocese when he met her in the Olympic Stadium in Seoul. He sent his classmate to escort her party to his diocese. We were met at the airport by a delegation of priests and laity with bouquets of flowers. When we arrived at Bishop Kim's home, he brought us into his private chapel and thanked God "for bringing Eileen George to his diocese, the smallest, poorest, and least in Korea." His eighteen priests and his sisters then gathered to hear Mrs. George speak.

The next day four thousand gathered to hear her. Although Catholics on Cheju Island number only twenty-seven thousand, the crowd swelled to seven thousand during the day as more and more people got out of work and school. Here and throughout Korea, Eileen encouraged people to frequent the sacraments, sharing with them her inability to survive without the daily Eucharist. To fall deeply in love, one needs to spend time with a person, and so it is with falling deeply in love with Jesus. Spend time with Him in the Eucharist, in prayer, thinking often of Him during the day, go to the Sacrament of Reconciliation which opens the spiritual doors of the soul.

13.3 The Love for Eileen

The Koreans showed their great love for Eileen by their applause. They greeted her by clapping and bouquets of flowers wherever she appeared, even as she approached the building in which she was going to speak. They applauded the healings with joy. The bishops and priests were astonished by the gift of knowledge by which she called out the healings. In Cheju Island she called out a healing for "a man with glasses in the upper balcony" whom she couldn't see, and suddenly he stood up. She called out a healing of the back and knees of a woman in front of her "with purple pants." An old woman in white stood up, and pulling up her traditional Korean dress showed her purple pants. Mrs. George went into a fit of laughing and the bishop almost fell off his chair in amazement.

Eileen closed the service with a word of prophesy, a message of Daddy God to His children, "My beloved children, I have gathered you here to praise and worship your God. You are not here by chance. I have tapped ever so gently on your hearts. I have brought you here so I could touch you in a very special way and I have touched all of you. I have enkindled in your hearts a new flame of burning love for your God and for each other. I promise you, you will never be the same again, for truly this day God has visited His people. Your prayers have risen like fresh incense to My throne and in return I have showered you with graces and blessings. This island will be known as an island of true Christian love."

Some healings confirming Eileen's ·message were public. Some were unnoticed, as happened in the sports complex at Taegu. A man with fingers bent and frozen to his palm reached out to her in the crowded hallway as we were leaving. She stopped a second, touched the man's hand, and he opened it, freely moving all his fingers.

Two scripture passages were often on Eileen's lips. One was, "Thou shalt not have strange gods before Me." But we do, we have little gods of our own: clothes, possessions, attitudes, our own will. By the prayer for openness to grace we can allow God to heal our hearts.

The other scripture passage was, "What does it profit one to gain the whole world and lose one's soul." We can't bring our possessions with us, no moving truck accompanies us to the cemetery. But we can store up our acts of love and fidelity to the duties of our state of life.

13.4 The Price of Working for the Kingdom

Koreans work from sunrise to sunset. High school students bring their lunch and supper to school. Class does not end until late in the evening. Mrs. George urged the priests and sisters to work hard for the kingdom, saying that the fruit of their work could not be taken from them, but will be waiting for them. She exhorted them to be great lovers, like Daddy God, who looking upon His Son in the manger, became so soft and gentle. This is the Father who wants to reveal Himself to us, so that like Him, we can become great lovers. He in turn will give us the Holy Spirit, the Lover of our souls. She urged them not to settle for anything less, explaining to them the mystical cycle. First fall deeply in love with Jesus, Jesus will bring you to the Father, and the Father will give you the Spirit, who will bring you to Jesus with greater love than ever, filled with knowledge, wisdom and understanding. So the cycle goes on.

Eileen paid a heavy price. There is nothing glamorous about this kind of a ministry. Illness, fatigue, loss of sleep and appetite were her portion, in addition to the burden of cancer, with the resultant loss of immunity to infection. She offers it all that people may come to know the Father. Her many acts of self-sacrifice brought blessings to God's people, strengthening the faith of the Korean Church.

13.5 At the Mount of the Beheaded

On the way to the airport for my return flight, a few days before hers, we stopped at the Mount of the Beheaded, the Martyr's Shrine for St. Andrew Kim, the young Korean priest martyr who encourages Eileen's apostolate among the Korean people. We asked Eileen the until-now unknown site of St. Andrew's martyrdom. As she pointed to the spot, beyond the beach in the water, once shore, her face and complexion are transformed and glow. She seems to be seeing something we could not see, and for a moment is out of contact with us.

As we leave the Shrine, she says she saw Andrew Kim standing over the spot of his martyrdom, a very young man about five foot six inches tall, not the most handsome of the Koreans, but with a glow that made his face beautiful. In time there will be a sign there which will bring many Koreans to the Faith.

She also saw his martyrdom. She saw a man with a band around his head on an animal like an ox, smaller than a horse. This animal had a blanket over it marked with a symbol composed of two horizontal lines and under it a square. The man had an instrument like a sickle. As he approached Andrew Kim, buried up to his neck in the sand, his face being eaten by large insects, the man on the animal passed with the sickle between her and Andrew so she could not see the beheading.

Previously Andrew had told her that just as his head was to be cut off, he had seen the Blessed Mother and had gone into a rapture. The glow on Mrs. George's face during this experience made her beautiful and left no room for further questions. Daddy God had certainly visited His people.

(Fr. James Caldarella is pastor of Prince of Peace Church, Princeton, Mass. This article was printed in the Worcester Catholic Free Press.)

19. Eileen with Archbishop Juan Dias, Apostolic Pro-Nuncio to Korea.

20. 30,000 fill the Olympic Gymnastic Stadium to hear Eileen in 1989

21. Fr. James Caldarella blesses Eileen before her service in his church.

Chapter Fourteen
God In America

14.1 God has Blessed America

"Is God in America and not in other countries? I thought God was everyplace." Yes, you're right. God is everywhere. But I'm talking about God in America. God is present in America and we sense Him, we acknowledge Him. On our coins we put, "In God We Trust." In our songs of state and country we sing, "God Bless America, bless our country."

People from all over the world desire to come to America. We are not ashamed to proclaim to the other nations that there is a God and we are calling on Him to bless America. And He has blessed America. So we are the land of plenty, the land of the free.

In America, if you're Catholic, Protestant, Non-Christian, Jew, you may worship God as you please. We have freedom of worship. And who made America free? God, because we called upon Him as a nation to bless us, to keep His hand of protection upon us. That is what made America great.

We are one of the first countries to reach out our hand to our brothers because we have plenty. And who gave us this plenty? Almighty God. Regardless of color, race or creed, we acknowledge God as our Father, our great provider. Take "In God We Trust" off the coins, and yes, my friends, you will see a great difference. It will be one of the darkest days of our country. Take the hymns away that praise Almighty God, and there will be a great difference in this land.

14.2 Leaders

If you search the history of our presidents, you will find that each one was a God-fearing man. There were no atheists among them. We are blessed in our presidents. God blesses America, because we bless Him by acknowledging His presence, by praising Him, by trusting Him. God honors us because we honor Him. You can see the fruits of His blessings upon us.

A leader of a foreign country finds his leadership is failing, his country seems to be going down the drain. Let him turn his country over to God, and say, "O God, please help us." Let him ask his people to request the help of Almighty God, and I guarantee there will be a great change in that country. He will no longer have strife. There will be peace once more in that country and he will govern gloriously, because he has committed himself and his country to the Supreme Being, God Almighty.

If a country is failing, it's because the people, the subjects of that country, allow their leaders to play God: they look up to this human as to a king. This is not right. God has given the ruler his or her command. The ruler must acknowledge this leadership as a gift coming from Almighty God, and he must ask for God's daily grace to help him to rule his or her country in the best manner. Then the blessings of Almighty God will flourish among the people. "Render to God what is God's, and render to Caesar what is Caesar's." You cannot run a country without God Almighty. You may think you can, but try calling upon God Almighty, and His help, and your land will flourish. The kingdom of Almighty God shall once more reign in your country. Look into it and see if this is not the truth.

14.3 Leaders Must Search Their Souls

Leaders of a country that push God out of their country will work for man and with man's evil grabbiness for possession of other people's land and countries. If they do not have God, they are miserable. They'll start war after war. A God-fearing, God-loving leader, king, president, or governor will bring peace into his land – not frustration and conflict. God is a God of love and unity, peace and harmony, not of division.

If a leader tries to divide his country, or to strike out against other countries, then he is not a man of God, he is working for the spirit of darkness and his only aim is possession, lust, grabbiness. A God-fearing-loving leader will want peace and prosperity for his people, and this is not gained by fighting his brother in another country, by trying to take land that does not belong to him. God is a God of unity and peace. The leaders must search their very souls and see if this is the leadership they are giving to their subjects. Would they be willing to put upon their coin, "In God We Trust"? It takes a man to proclaim to the world that he acknowledges his God as the Supreme Being and that he is His subject. A coward turns his back on God.

Our leaders proclaim to the world that they are God-fearing people. They want peace and unity. That's why I say, "God in America." For God is truly in our great country, the land of peace and of the free. The land whose people are not ashamed to proclaim to all countries and to cry out, "God in Heaven, bless our country, bless America. We want you to know in God we trust, we put it on our coins."

14.4 Harmony with God and Each Other: Dedication to God

Our religious leaders, Catholic, Orthodox, Christians, Non-Christians, Jews, of every race, color or creed, reach out to each other in the sign of peace. They help one another; they love one another. At times they have disagreements, its true, but this is our humanness. Most of our ministers, Catholic priests and rabbis are friendly and love one another. They go separate ways in their worship of God, but it is the same God they are worshipping, and their heart is in their way of worship. This is unity and peace. Catholics are not killed because they are Catholics, Protestants because they are Protestants, or Jews because they are Jews. God's reign shows. It shows on our faces.

We wake up in the morning and look out the window at the birds flying free. We see the wind gently blowing through the trees, and we realize, "I am free. I am free as the bird and the wind because I live here in America." I look up to the heavens and I say, "O God, thank you for granting me to live in America, the land of the free. Thank You for giving me this great gift." It makes me stop and think and pray for countries that are not as free as we are. Yes, God is here in America because we dedicate ourselves to Him, to God our Almighty Father.

God looks down upon the peoples of the world as His children, but He wonders, "Why have you not dedicated yourselves and your country to Me? I want to shower My blessings upon you, but you must voluntarily dedicate your country to Me, Creator of the heavens and the earth. Is this asking too much of My children? If you want to be prosperous, children all over the world, dedicate your lives to the Heavenly Father. I give freedom, prosperity, and peace. All I ask is that you come to Me and acknowledge your God."

In walking the streets of America there is an air of freedom, of joy, and of peace. You do not feel restrained. You're free flowing, free sailing, free in the Spirit because you know that God is watching over you. There is a presence here in America that you may not be able to find everywhere. Yes, God is everywhere, He is in every country. But He must be acknowledged. If you do not give Him this acknowledgement you will not feel free, easy, and peaceful. You must dedicate yourself to Him. He will not invade the free will or the freeness of any country. Each must offer loyalty and love to the Heavenly Father freely.

Even the sound of America brings peace and joy to souls throughout the world. In the sound of the name, there is a peacefulness, a tranquility within the soul. Why? God reigns in America, and He puts this peace and tranquility in the name *America*. Land of the free, land of God Almighty. There is something about America, and that something is God Almighty.

14.5 Our Taxes

Some people say we are heavily taxed, but are we now? Do not our taxes pay for the policeman to protect us, thousands and thousands and thousands of policemen? Don't they come to your door at your beck and call? Are you paying them? Through taxes. Is this not just? And what about the firemen? Who is paying their salary? It's your taxes. So you see, your money is not lost. And what about your beautiful streets? Everyone has to chip in, they are for your personal use. You can use any street in the country, except for a small toll charge on some of the expressways. But is it such a great thing to pay a tax for this freedom? You can come and go as you please. You can walk the streets and the beautiful sidewalks. And what about the litter? Men have to be paid to pick up the litter, to keep America beautiful.

Aren't you proud of your country? Don't you want nice streets? Aren't you proud of the police that protect you? And the firemen who also endanger their lives for you? And the beautiful buildings. You have many things to thank God for, can you not share a little of your money in taxes to pay the government? I am probably the poorest of all. Being the mother of eight children makes me wonder at times about the taxes. Then I sit down and have a talk with my God, and I realize, it is just, it is right. It hurts us once in awhile, but we live in America, in the land of the free, and we must take care of it the best we can with our taxes. My beloved friends, is this too great a price to pay for living in this country where God reigns? Give it a little honest to goodness thought. Where man has an equal opportunity, and equal rights, where we grant men and women from other countries a right equal to ours. Why do we do it? Because we're American people and we attribute all our luxury, our peace, our freedom to God. God blesses America.

14.6 A Prayer

Let's bow our head in prayer, holding hands, spiritually, as brothers and sisters, regardless of color, race or creed, as Americans, God-loving people. "Heavenly Father, each and every one of us kneel before Thee and we look up into Thy face. And as You cup our faces in Your hands, Heavenly Father, and search our very souls, we say, Father, we give You our thanks. We thank and we praise You for having given us to live here in America, the land of plenty, the land of the free. We thank You, Heavenly

Father, for giving us the grace to call Your blessings down upon America. Father God, we thank You for giving us the grace to put 'In God We Trust' upon our coins. May we never lose the image of our Heavenly Father. Father we ask You to continue to bless our beautiful country and to give us Your peace and joy. Give us the brotherly love that our souls desire. Give us the charity to reach out to foreign countries in peace and love and to bring to them the true understanding of a peaceful, God-fearing-loving nation, a nation in which we say God is our Supreme Being, we trust fully in Him, for He is our God.

"Heavenly Father, Father of us all, of every country, of every state, we thank Thee for being our God. We thank Thee most of all for being our Heavenly Father, and we ask you to bring this same peace we enjoy to every country of the world. We praise You, Heavenly Father, and we ask Your blessings upon this, our beautiful country, America."

PART FIVE

LAST THINGS

Chapter Fifteen

The Plateaus of Heaven

15.1 The Levels

God wants to reveal His kingdom to you in the quietness of your day. We don't know about the kingdom of Heaven. When I was a little child I thought – and my own children have said this to me, my sons especially –"Heaven must be a dull place if all you do is pray there." Almost, "I don't want to go." This is what people think. That's because we haven't learned to communicate with God so He can reveal His kingdom to us. In Heaven they praise, they worship, but they don't pray [petition]. They've gotten as far as they're going to get.

In Heaven there are different plateaus. There's not just one place, "I'm in Heaven." "I'm in Purgatory." "I'm in Hell." There are different levels of Hell. There are different levels of Purgatory. It stands to reason. If somebody obeys the commandments of God, and this is good, obeys the precepts of the Church and goes to Mass on Sunday under pain of sin, as an obligation, and tries to be a good Christian, that much, and does not try to practice virtue beyond that, he or she certainly will get into the kingdom of Heaven, right? But say his neighbor or her neighbor tries every day to go to Mass because she or he wants to, (I have to keep saying "he" and "she" because I don't want to be labelled, so if I forget to put in a "he" or a "she" please don't throw daggers at me), tries to go to Mass every day of his or her life because they want to draw closer to Jesus. He or she tries to make acts of charity for the poor, and helps the sick, the afflicted, and tries so hard to be a virtuous, holy person. Naturally, he or she isn't going to go into the first level, this person is going to climb to a higher level.

According to the spiritual life that you lead on earth, that's the level you'll get to in the kingdom. As long as you have a breath in you, you can try for the Seventh Heaven. Beyond that are the Father, Jesus and the angels. But as long as you try to be the best person ever, do acts of kindness and love, and stay close to Jesus, you can climb to the Seventh Heaven.

15.2 Happiness in the Different Plateaus

Will the person on the first level be happy? Completely happy, because that's what he or she earned, obeying the commandments of God, the precepts of the Church, obeying all the rules. They're perfectly happy and content and they see God as much as He allows them to see Him on the first level. The second plateau sees God in a more full way and this is so on each plateau. It's like a thimble, a quart bottle, and a jug. The thimble is the first level of the kingdom. The thimble is filled to its capacity. The thimble doesn't say to the quart bottle, "I'm jealous, you're holding more." "I'm filled," the thimble says, "to my capacity." And if you enter the first plateau, evidently that's your capacity. But while we have a chance, while we still have a breath within us, we must strive to be a better person every day of our life, more Christ-like, so we can enter way up into the seventh plateau, and see God to a greater degree.

I see the Father in a human form as I see you, but there are veils between the Father and me. Every once in awhile I say to the Father, "You look more beautiful today, my Father, than yesterday." I don't see the veil, but I know a veil has passed away. And the Father just looks at me and smiles. Even though I see the Father fully, it's not His fullness. Do you understand what I'm saying? The more I grow in my spiritual life, the more veils slip away from the Father. We want to see as much as we can of the Father.

15.3 Perfect Happiness

If you enter the first plateau of Heaven, you'll be perfectly and completely happy. There is no jealousy in the kingdom. You won't be able to go to the second, third, fourth, or the seventh plateau, this is it. But you will have a rich, full, beautiful life. If you go to the second level of Heaven, you'll be able to come down and visit the first level, but those on the second level cannot go to the third level. If you go to the Seventh Heaven, because you were extra good, and extra special, and cooperated with grace, and really worked hard, you can come down and visit all the plateaus of the kingdom.

So we should try to sit in the peace of our bedroom, our parlor, our car, wherever, and try to get closer to the Lord, so we'll begin to hunger and thirst and strive for the Seventh Heaven. Maybe we won't reach it, but always try to aim high. We may fall a little below, but at least we're trying to aim high. Each plateau has all the fringe benefits and beauties of our loving Father. Heaven is a beautiful place, a wonderful place.

15.4 Where is Heaven?

I once said to Daddy God, "My Father, where is Heaven?" And He said to me, "Why do you ask, Child?" I said, "Father, so many people tell me different things. I said to a priest, 'Father, where's Heaven?' He said, 'Oh, it's behind a cloud.' I asked someone else and he said, 'Heaven is in a hidden valley.' Other people gave me different answers." I said, "Father, I'm confused, where is Heaven?" Now you can call it a revelation, you can call it a dream. I call it a dream. My spiritual director calls it a revelation. I don't like to use those terms, I'm a very simple person. Call it anything you want. The Father said to me, "Hold my hand, Child, I will take you there." And I held my Father God's hand, and we stepped from my back stairs into a new dimension.

It's like stepping over a line, and that's Heaven. This land is very beautiful. There are no telephone poles, buildings, cars, roads. I saw valleys, I saw mountains, I saw streams. I saw beautiful trees and flowers. As the Father and I walked hand in hand, the trees bowed, like willows, in humble adoration to the

Father. The flowers nodded in reverence. Never on this earth, nor in the florists, have I seen such flowers, nor such colors. They weren't blue, yellow, green nor orange, I can't describe them. The aroma from those flowers would put you in ecstasy. I've never on earth smelled this aroma.

15.5 The Wolf and the Lamb Lie Down Together

There was no fighting. You know how a wolf will eat a lamb on earth. I saw the wolf eating with the lamb and lying down with the lamb. Everything was in peace and harmony. I saw babbling brooks and as they went over the rocks, they were singing a melodious tune to the Father. As we approached the stream, little fishes came above the water and nodded to the Father. The peace and reverence was unbelievable. Everything acknowledged the Father in this land called Heaven.

15.6 Eating in Heaven!

I saw fruit trees. If anyone tells you that it's dull in Heaven, no, we will eat. We will eat to enjoy, not to survive. The trees were loaded with fruit. The Father saw me looking at the fruit and He said, "Pick a fruit, Child." I couldn't tell you if it was a pear, a peach or a plum, it was some kind of, I call it, exotic fruit. Every time I go to the market I look to see if there is anything that looks like the Father's fruit. But there never is.

I picked the fruit as the Father suggested and I bit into it. It was the sweetest, the most delicious fruit I have ever tasted. Then the Father said, "Look back at the branch." And when I looked, where I had picked the fruit, there was another fruit. I said, "Father, I just picked that fruit, what is it doing there?" He said, "Child, I've been with you so often, don't you know the time here is always now?" Otherwise I'd say, "There used to be a fruit there." Past tense. Time in the kingdom is always present. So you see the beauty that's awaiting us. There is eating in the kingdom, but you won't find meat nor fish to eat. There's no killing of animals in the kingdom.

15.7 **The Reverence of God's Creatures**

As I walked with the Father, birds flew, as though they knew He was coming, and they all gathered around the Father's and my head, and their wings touched, like they were playing ring around the rosy. As they flew around the Father's head and around my head, they sang the most melodious tune I have ever heard. The birds were beautiful.

My yard is like a game sanctuary. I have every kind of bird, but I've never seen these birds. Talk about birds of paradise! Father Falco's father brought me some bird houses. I took a ladder and I put it against a tree; I no sooner had the birdhouse nailed to the tree than it was rented! They were carrying stuff into it before I came down. I have loads of birds in the yard, and squirrels, chipmunks, rabbits and God knows what else, but I've never seen birds like the birds in Heaven. I couldn't tell you what colors they are. They are all different sizes. I saw a beautiful animal, like a deer, but it wasn't a deer. It bounded out of the woods, and it bowed before the Father. It didn't bow before me, and it didn't speak to me, but when it looked at me with its big eyes, I heard the words with the ears of my soul, "And I love you too, welcome." This is only a little bit, the top frosting, of this wonderful place, Heaven. My spiritual director said it can all be traced back to Scripture. "Eyes have not seen, nor ears heard, the things I have prepared for you."

There is no light in the sky like the sun or the moon, the only light is the light of God. There are different choirs of angels, praising, worshipping and adoring. They give glory to God. When the Father had me step into our dimension to come back to our world, I said to Him, "Father, how is it that Your world doesn't collide with our world?" He said, "Because it's guided by the divine Holy Spirit." Heaven is not way up there, it's just stepping over a line into a new dimension. Many people say, "O Eileen, you're in a plane all the time, you're way up with God." I'm with God down here too. That's the way we were reared and geared: "God is way up there." God is here, inside of us, surrounding us.

15.8 The Valley

I'm trying to whet your spiritual appetites for the kingdom because I want you to realize there's so much more after this world. I believe with all my heart that now is the time to sit down and take notice of what God is preparing for you. Many times in my communions, dreams, or whatever you want to call them, the Father takes me to a valley, which hopefully I will reach by grace and acceptance of grace. I see new things in this valley which God is preparing for me, and I say, "Father, why wasn't that stream there when I was here yesterday?" And He says, "Spiritually you weren't ready to see that stream."

The better I become, the more beauty is revealed to me in my kingdom. Once I went there after Eucharist in my love time with Jesus, and I saw some little animals, babies, and I said, "Aha! I got you now, Father. How come there are little animals here if the time is always now? When were they born?" He said to me, "Eileen, I know you love little animals, so I put them there. They'll always be small for you, and you'll always enjoy them." You see how well He prepares the place that we are going to? He wants you to beautify it; the more you practice virtue, the more things He reveals to you. That stream wasn't there because I still had veils before my eyes that had to be dropped by acts of virtue.

15.9 Every Day is a New Awakening

Every time I go into my valley after receiving the Eucharist, it's a new awakening; it becomes more and more beautiful. I'm trying very hard to be a better person. If I don't see something new in that valley, I know that I'm at a standstill, so I try very hard to grow before I receive Jesus and go into my valley again.

Heaven is an exciting place. Death is the doorknob that we must turn to enter into everlasting life, peace and beauty. We fear to turn the doorknob because we don't know Heaven. If we knew Heaven, we would be excited about going there. We're all so human. I am human too. I look at my little grandkids, and I say, "God, you know how excited I am to come to you, but I think they need me now." They're kind of my stumbling blocks to the kingdom. He'll say, "You'll come in My time, not your time, Child."

15.10 My Black Stallion Midnight

I once had a black stallion. Believe it or not I used to be an expert horsewoman. I won many blue ribbons with him. His name was Midnight. He was bigger than a quarter horse, about eight inches above a quarter horse. He was a real stallion. I loved him dearly. He became very old and we had to put him out to pasture. Every day I would run down and spend time with him and with the Lord. One day I noticed he was lying down too much so I put him in the barn and we didn't let him out anymore, except for walks. Then, he wouldn't get up. I had to call the vet. The vet said he was dying. I cried and I cried and I, mother of eight children, threw myself on the bed and said, "O God, please, Father, give my horse life. Don't take him from me." I fell asleep crying. When I woke up my husband came in and said Midnight was dead.

15.11 I Got Angry with the Father

I got so angry with the Father. "You don't listen to me, Father. You don't love me."

"What's bringing this on, Child?"

"You know everything, You know what's bringing it on. Midnight's dead."

"Wait a minute. What happened?"

"I asked You, and I was crying, to give my Midnight life. You gave him death."

"No. I gave him real life. When you finally turn that doorknob of death, he will be in your valley waiting for you. He's alive. He's running now in the valley. You asked me to give him life, I gave him real life."

Many times since, in my love time with Jesus, I've seen Midnight running and prancing in the valley that I will come to when I turn that doorknob of death. You'll say, "Did the horse earn Heaven?" No. But I'm earning Heaven by grace and acceptance of grace and God will give me everything my heart desires including my black stallion, Midnight. He's there waiting for me. See what a wonderful God? The horse doesn't earn the kingdom, we do, and God gives us everything outside of sin that our hearts desire. What a tender, gentle and loving God! If only we give Him a chance to be our loving God, our Father.

15.12 Death not the Finale, but the Beginning

Death isn't the finale, it's the beginning of a rich, new life in the Lord Jesus Christ. This life is going through the motions of living. When I'm with the Father, that's life, and that's what I want you to understand. Heaven is a beautiful place, but you won't understand this, you'll hear Eileen's words and you may get her tape on Heaven, but you have to spend quiet times with our loving Father, with His divine Son. You have to hunger and thirst as the hind thirsts after the running waters. You have to pant after the things of God. The rosaries, Mass, which is the greatest prayer of all, all these things could very well just be outward signs because you're in the habit of doing them routinely, without spirituality.

You can be touched by these things, you can use them as stepping stones to the kingdom. You can find out what your real purpose is. "Am I doing things because I want people to see me?" Then, it says in Scripture, you'll get your reward from the people. But the reward for anything you do in secret for the love of God waits for you in the kingdom. So let's try to beautify the valley that God is preparing for us. He says, "In my Father's house there are many castles." There are many plateaus in the kingdom. While you still have breath, the gift of life, use it wisely and try to strive for the seventh plateau of the kingdom.

15.13 Striving

I hunger to be with God. When I was in the hospital after my four surgeries in two weeks for cancer, the prayer people used to come and pray over me. They would press so hard on my head, I thought it was going to go through my shoulders into my stomach. They would say, "O God, heal her. Heal her. Let her live one hundred years." And I'd say in my heart, "O God, don't listen to them!" In fact, there was one time when I wanted to go to the Father so badly, a song sprung from my heart, "Let me go to my Father. He wants me by His side. Please let me go. Don't tie me here. Free me and let me go." It was a beautiful song. I received it first in tongues and then in English. "Let me go to my Father. Please don't hold me here." And God love them, through their love for me and their spiritual life, they were trying to hold me here. Now I see God had another plan for me.

Once you know God in your quiet moments, you'll hunger for Him. Not that you'll say "I want to die tonight." I would love to die tonight but He's keeping me around awhile, probably for penance. But the idea is, Heaven is beautiful. I don't want you to wish for death, but to say, "God, help me to beautify my soul."

When I'm on my death bed, I'll be so excited, I hope, to go to God. But you better be careful, you never know how the old boy works with you at the hour of death. I think I'll be so excited about going to the Father. If there's a split second of sadness in me, I think it will be because I can no longer try for a higher place. This is it, kid, your time for virtue and grace is over, you're going to Him. Why not strive now for the kingdom, while we still have life and vitality and God's graces are flowing into our souls? Not doing great big things, extraordinary things, and all that stuff. Little things. The best thing you can do is to love one another. Sit in the quiet moments of your home and talk to Him. Say, "Father, I don't understand too much the spiritual life, help me. Open the spiritual eyes of my soul that I may see everything that You want me to see."

15.14 Christian Life is So Rich

I want you all to hunger after Him, to realize there's so much more to being a Christian. Sure, if you start with coming to Mass on Sunday, going to confession every couple of months or once a year, it's going to seem like a dull life being a Christian. But a Christian life is so rich, so exciting. Every day of my life, and I mean every day of my life, is a new awakening in God's love. No matter what the hardships, the trials or the sufferings, there is a new teaching there for me and I become excited over it. God wants to teach us, just as we want to teach our grandchildren how to walk right, how to talk right, how to say their prayers. God is the greatest of all parents, and He wants to teach us the spiritual life, but our mind is so congested with everything else, we don't give God a chance. He doesn't want to reveal His kingdom just to Eileen. He loves you. He, the Lord Jesus Christ, died for you as He died for me. He hungers for you as He hungers for me. He loves you as He loves me. So you see, He wants to reveal His kingdom to all of us, if we only give Him a chance. He's blessed us with these wonderful seasons of the liturgical year to get our lives together, to come away for awhile into our own little garden of Gethsemane and pray with Him. Ask God to open your mind, to give you the grace of openness, to be open to everything that He wants to reveal to you by His grace and your acceptance of grace.

15.15 Practice A Little Virtue

Always pray for the grace of openness. Practice a little virtue. My husband came home last night and he said, "Mommy's too sweet on the phone. What is she up to, Colleen?" Colleen said, "It's Lent, Daddy. It's Lent." He didn't even have his first cup of coffee and he wants to know what's for supper. So you see, I have to struggle. You have to struggle to become holy. No matter how long you've lived with someone, you get on each other's nerves sometimes and instead of whiplashing out, be twice as kind. It's not easy. Be twice as loving to beautify this valley of yours.

Now I'm on the husband thing. The other night we were having coffee, and he said, "Mommy, will you make me some coffee?"

I said, "Sure Dad, I just made some in the dripulator."

"I like coffee perked on the stove."

I should have taken the drip, poured it into the coffee pot and said, "Here." He wouldn't have known the difference. He's really a good man. I made the coffee and by that time I didn't want any.

Afterwards I said, "Gee Dad, you're not having your coffee."

"You didn't hand me the sugar."

I said, "Daddy, if I went outside for an hour, would you keep that cup of coffee until I came back and handed you the sugar?"

I'm terrible, I'm far from perfect. But you see what I'm trying to say? He's a saint. I'm pushing him way up there. When I die, I'm going to say, "Hey Dad, what are you doing up there?"

He's going to say, "You pushed me up here; living with you."

Chapter Sixteen

Questions and Answers:
My first Meeting with the Father

At a retreat Eileen invited questions, saying: "Feel free to raise your hand and if I possibly can, with the light of the Holy Spirit, I'll try to answer your questions. O.K.?"

16.1 Question: "How did you come to know the Father?"

Eileen: "There was a time when I didn't know my Father. I shiver at the thought. I knew Jesus since I was a little girl. I had a very close walk since the age of three, maybe since two and a half. I went through a growing up stage with Him, as my big brother. I went through the mystical courtship, I went through the mystical marriage. But I didn't know the Father. And I was like a daughter-in-law fighting with her in-laws. 'Jesus, I love You, I adore You, who's Your Father?' And that went on for many years. I went to a priest and I said, 'Father, I want to love God the Father, the First Person, who is He?' He showed me a cloud with wings. Meaning a spirit. 'This is your Father.' I couldn't relate to that. I went to another priest and I said, 'Who's the Father?' He showed me an old man above the altar, and he looked like Rip Van Winkle, with a long long beard, and he said, 'That's the Father.' I said, 'O God, that's why I don't love the Father.' I couldn't relate to that father. My father was clean shaven, he was a very handsome man. So my constant gripe was, 'Butchie, who's Your Father?' That went on for years.

"I had many priests coming to my home. One day, I said, 'Well, I'm going to take a vacation, I'm going way down the

backyard. None of the priests will know where I am. I'll hide
there and sit and talk to God.' So I went back by the pine trees,
and I sat in a chair, and I said, 'Nobody will find me here.' I say, I
fell asleep. My spiritual director says other things. I was
complaining, 'Who's Your Father?' And in the dream, or
whatever, I heard a voice say, 'Eileen, Eileen.' And I said, 'O my
God one of my priests found me, I'll play possum. I'm not
opening my eyes.' Then I heard the voice saying, 'Eileen, stop
being silly, open those eyes.' I said to myself, 'Gee, that doesn't
sound like any of my priests.'

"I opened my eyes and there I saw the most beautiful man
that I have ever seen. He was sitting on a throne, wearing kingly
attire, made of light. It looked like material but when you went to
touch it, your hands went through it. I looked up at Him, and He
had the most beautiful face with the ruddiest skin I have ever
seen. He looked like He was in the sun all the time, not just for a
week. And His eyes were the bluest eyes. And when I looked at
Him, I could feel my heart throbbing and beating so fast. He was
clean shaven, no mustache, no beard. His hair was white, like
spun silk, falling in very soft waves to His shoulders, not matted.
Inside I felt like He was the Father. I fell in love with Him
immediately. But always suspicious, I said, 'Who is it?' He said,
'Eileen, I'm the Father, I love you so much, I took a form so you
could love me. I'm God, I can do anything I want.' My mind
started racing into Scripture. Right, He took a form in Scripture.
It says, 'I saw Him sitting on a throne.' Now if He was sitting on a
throne, He had something to sit with. 'In His right hand He
held . . . ' well if He had a right hand, I'm sure He had a left
hand. So inside, I'm saying, Yes, He can take a form if He wants.
Then another question arose. 'O.K., if your the Father how come
you don't look like your kid?' Jesus has hazel eyes, auburn hair.
And the Father went like this. I said, 'No I don't mean the beard. I
mean He's completely different looking from You.' Listen to this
closely, my spiritual director said He gave me the greatest
theology in a nutshell. He said, 'Why Eileen, Butchie doesn't
look like Me, because He has only the genes of Mary.' Jesus looks

like Mary. That's the answer. So we should hunger, thirst, fall deeply and madly in love with Jesus so He'll lead us to our Father."

16.2 Question: "Would you tell me what Purgatory is like?"

Eileen: "Honey, I don't know too much about Purgatory. I know about Heaven and I certainly know about Hell. I once asked my Father about Purgatory, and here's the answer He gave me, 'Eileen, from the moment you come from your mother's womb, the first slap is the beginning of your purgatory.'

"It's a place where you have to go to be purged. Even though we confess our sins, we hurt an infinite God, there should be a purification either on this earth or whatever. If you hurt your mother you say, Mother I'm sorry, please forgive me. She certainly does forgive you, but she's still hurting inside, so you try to make it up to her. God is a loving God, He's all pure and all holy, and the real example is Jesus Christ dying upon the Cross. An infinite God was hurt, an infinite God had to pay the price.

"I believe with all my heart that we can lessen our purgatory. Everything we're going through here in our life, me with cancer, you with headaches, or heartbreak with children – offer it up to reduce your time in Purgatory. O.K.? And that's all I know. God has never revealed this place to me."

16.3 Question: "Something that has always bothered me is, Why God allows Satan to have so much power?"

Eileen: "Easy. How are we going to gain Heaven, become virtuous, if we don't have something to fight? For instance, the devil could say to God, and on one occasion maybe he did, Sure, Eileen loves you. You're her Daddy. You always have your arms around her, protecting her. Withdraw from Eileen and give me a chance. We'll see how much she loves you.' And then the proof is in the pudding. 'I prove I love you, Father, with my whole heart and soul. Get behind me, Satan.' Do you understand?

"Even Jesus was tempted. How are we going to merit the kingdom of Heaven without temptation? We have to work for the kingdom. You know, that's one thing about Protestantism, they'll say, 'Jesus did it all!' No, He didn't, He wouldn't be a just God. Jesus opened the gates of Heaven. We have to earn entrance into the kingdom, and one of the ways of earning it is by rebuking Satan. O.K.?"

16.4 Question: "Is there a danger in letting people pray over you?"

Eileen: "I think there is, but I'm not a great Philadelphia theologian. I'm very careful who lays hands on me, or touches me. Not because I think I'm better than anyone, but I am the temple of the Holy Spirit. Not that they're beneath me, no, never would I think that. But I believe you have to be careful who lays hands on you. Sometimes there are eager beavers and they're not pushed by the good spirit."

16.5 Question: "In a prayer, they refer to God as 'She.' "

Eileen: "Jesus said, 'Our Father,' masculine. 'I have come to reveal the Father.' He didn't say, 'I've come to reveal the Mother.' The Father has the gentleness, the tenderness of a mother, but He's masculine. O.K., sweetheart?

16.6 Question: "If you're praying for a soul that died and is in Heaven, what happens to those prayers?"

Eileen: "God uses them for another soul that has no one to pray for it. And I'll tell you something, and I didn't mean to get into this. I had to drive my husband to work because we only had one car, and as I drove him to work, it was about five in the morning, I looked down onto the expressway, and there was a truck overturned. You could tell the driver was dead. Now there's a teaching here, please listen.

"I drove my husband to the shop, and when I came back, they still were trying to get him out. I went home, and almost four hours later, I was driving some of the children to school, and I looked over onto the expressway, and they still hadn't gotten the man out. So I picked my beads off the dash and I started saying them for this man, dead hours ago. And as I started saying the beads, the Father spoke to me, 'Because of your beads, this man is in the kingdom.'

" 'Father, how can this man be in the kingdom? He was dead hours before I picked up my beads.'

"'The grace of anticipation. From the beginning of time, I knew you were going to pray for him. So I applied that grace ahead of time.'

'Do you understand? And 'Hail Mary, full of grace,' how could she be full of grace? Jesus had not died to win the graces yet. The grace of anticipation. What a wonderful God we have. So keep praying, and if that person's in Heaven, God just uses those wonderful prayers and sacrifices and applies them to another soul. O.K.? Never stop praying. Does that answer your question? Praise the Lord Jesus Christ."

16.7 Question: "Eileen, what happens to Jewish people who don't accept Jesus? Will they be saved? Did you ever talk to Jesus about what happens to the Jews when they die?"

Eileen: "You know our minds are very narrow as Catholics. My spiritual director once told me a joke. A Jew went to Heaven. He knocked at the gate: 'Peter, can I come in?"

" 'Why not?' Peter let him in. As they are walking around, they saw some people in a valley. The Jew said to Peter, 'Who are those beautiful people down there?'

" 'Ssh! They're Catholics. They think they're the only ones up here!'

"Yes. If a Jew believes with all his or her heart they're in the right faith, they certainly can get to Heaven. But if you have the slightest doubt, the slightest doubt, you're obligated to look into it. Understand? If you have the slightest doubt, it's God's grace touching you, pulling you in gently to inquire about the Faith. He's already working with you, and that's the biggest miracle of all.

"Father Feeney was a very wonderful man, but a little misguided. He was excommunicated but then later brought back into the Church by the grace of God. His theology was that only Catholics get to Heaven. Of course there are other people in Heaven besides us, but if you have the slightest doubt, you are obligated under sin, to look into it. O.K.?"

"You know my spiritual director is a Jew, a convert. His mother gave him an awful time. She died a Jewess in a Catholic nursing home. I never saw her in my life. He never described his mother. I went to sleep one night thinking about her, wondering about her being saved. In my dream I saw this lady. She was very small, very petite. She was running around moving furniture from one place to another. She was keeping herself very busy, never seeing me. I described her to a T to my director. And it was his mother. She was in the kingdom of Heaven."

16.8 Question: "Has Father God ever revealed to you about relatives in the kingdom?"

Eileen: "You'll know them, but there are no husbands, no wives, no parents. There is one bridegroom, the Lord Jesus Christ. There won't be any sadness."

16.9 Question: "There are reports of out-of-body experiences."

Eileen: "I don't get into out-of-body experiences, I don't get into Buddhism, I don't get into any of these things. I just get into loving the Lord and trying to stay ever so close to Him."

16.10 Question: "My husband is Jewish and he turned Catholic and I try to get him to go to church with me and he doesn't think not going is against the law."

Eileen: "But at least he had the grace to become a Catholic. Keep pursuing him by prayer and sacrifice. O.K.? And let God be his judge. Jesus appeared to Saint Margaret Mary. He spoke about priests, but I know He meant all of us. He said, 'Margaret, you are never to judge the priests. You are to love them. I will judge them.' And I think He means that about each one of us. Don't judge each other. Love each other and leave the judging to Him. O.K.?"

16.11 Question: "A child of four has Catholic parents but has never been baptized."

Eileen: "Well the sin is on the parents, it's their responsibility, not the child's. Perhaps when he is older he will ask for baptism. He may go to Heaven, but who says they will?"

16.12 Question: "Eileen, I have a neighbor, she doesn't know whether there's a God or not but she's a very good person. She's more Christian in her ways than people who claim to be Christian, and she isn't a Christian."

Eileen: "Only God can judge. I'm sure she knows God. There's such a thing as natural grace, and supernatural grace. I'm sure she knows God, and I'm sure God has placed her in your life so you can pray for her and be the mainstream of her salvation. O.K.?"

16.13 Question: "I have two sons that don't go to church. They went to Catholic schools. My oldest son tells me there is no God, that earth was created in an explosion. I pray every single day, every time I remember, for their conversion. Is there such a thing as nagging God?"

Eileen: "No. He delights in it. He delights in it. But you know what, kids, at a certain age, they need their space. Don't nag them. Scripture says, Don't excite your children to anger. Pursue them by prayer and sacrifice. You can never nag God. He delights in your being a nag. Keep after Him, He loves it. O.K.?"

16.14 Question: "How do you answer young people when they say they have big faith, but they don't believe in organized religion?"

Eileen: "It's a cop out. Just pray for them. Every organization, every family, has to be organized or else it falls apart. A house divided will fall. If he goes into a job, there are rules he has to obey. Policemen have to obey. Right? Nurses, doctors, families. They're all organized. We have to obey. It's a cop out. Pursue them by prayer. They'll come around, I promise you. O.K.? Look at Saint Monica. Thirty years. He came around. Augustine said, 'O Lord, I want to be converted, but not now. Come back another time.' "

16.15 Question: "Can you explain the process of healing, when you heal us?"

Eileen: "First of all, I don't heal you. God heals you. Sometimes it's gradual, because you need an inner healing. God is working in a spiritual way. Say a man has an alcohol problem. He's receiving a gradual healing because he needs the inner healing first. God isn't going to zap him out of his alcohol problem, he'll get into something else.

"I know a person in a wheel-chair, and he wants a healing, and I know God is never going to heal him physically, because if He did, he'd jump right out of that wheel-chair and lose his vocation. He's a little rascal. Sometimes God heals gradually, and sometimes He heals right on the spot.

"I get the word of knowledge. I hear my Father's voice. He'll say, 'See that pretty lady over there, that petite lady, she's being healed of this. Eileen, call it out.' So I point at you and say, 'You're being healed of this.' I hear His voice. He does the healing."

16.16 Question: "How clearly do you see Jesus?"

Eileen: "You are getting into my spiritual life! But that's all right. As clearly as I see you. I see my Father as I see you. But I know there are many veils between us. Every once in awhile I'll say to my Father, 'You look so handsome today, You're more beautiful than ever.' I know within my soul another veil has slipped away. There are many veils. I see Him as clearly as I see you, but not clearly enough to see His Godship. I see Jesus like I see you."

16.17 Question: "You said the Father, the Son and the Holy Spirit have different identities, right? And you said, that you have to pray to Jesus to know the Father?"

Eileen: "That's scripture."
"O.K. When we pray, do we pray to each identity, or do we pray to God, or to Jesus?"
Eileen: "You pray to Jesus to reveal His Father because of the Scripture, 'No one knows the Father except the Son, and those that He wishes to reveal Him to.' So if you want to get to know the Father, you certainly must go to Jesus, spend time with Him, love him, and in His time, He will reveal the Father. You can't skip over Jesus and get to the Father. It tells you so in Scripture. O.K.?"

16.18 Question: "Eileen, you refer to the Holy Spirit as Carsha?"

Eileen: "Carsha."
"What does that mean?"
Eileen: "Lover of thy soul. O.K.? You can use it."

16.19 Question: "You have spoken of the different levels of Heaven, what is the obstacle to our going to the highest level?"

Eileen: "It's ourself. We're filled with pride and jealousy and envy and self-ambition. We get very tired easily. We should shoot for the highest plateau. We may drop lower, but always aim for the highest plateau. Usually it's ourself that pulls us down. That's why I say, don't confuse your natural life with your mystical life with Christ. In our humanness we have attachments, and they weigh us down, and I don't want any attachments. So I have to cut them free so I can fly to the heights as you have to fly to the heights. Always aim high, we may reach it. As long as we have a breath in us, we can reach the Seventh Heaven. As long as we isolate ourself with God and His love. There's always hope. Now is the time to begin. Don't put it off till to-morrow. We may not have to-morrow."

16.20 **Question: "Would you explain a little more about detachment as far as our children are concerned."**

Eileen: "That's different. That's a human attachment, it's a distraction if it comes in your prayer. God understands about your worry about your children. But not to a point of getting frustrated, because then you're playing God. Kneel down or sit down and pray to God to take care of these children, if they have problems: drugs, alcohol, marriage or whatever. Pray for them and then give them to God. Say, God, I'll pray and I'll sacrifice.

"That's not a bad attachment. But be attached to them through prayer. You are not God. Place them in the Father's arms spiritually. Every once in a while we are going to take them back, because they are our children, but then say, God, please forgive me, you take care of them, I'll pray and I'll sacrifice for them. God expects you to be concerned. A bad attachment is one that takes you from God. We have to sever it and get rid of it."

16.21 **Question: "Explain the difference between meditation and contemplation."**

Eileen: "I'll try. There's praying out of a book. Then there is meditation, like when you look at our Lord upon the Cross, and think of all He has done for you. You are aware of what your doing. In contemplation, you get lost in a word, like Jesus, or in a subject, and you're oblivious. It's not ecstasy. Few reach it, but maybe God doesn't want it, He takes us all on a different path."

16.22 **Question: "Fr. Gobbi talked of difficulties coming."**

Eileen: "I don't like to comment on the difficulties that are coming. I take one day at a time. I try not to get into 'days of darkness' and all this stuff. I know what they say is true.

"Our Lord says, I come as a thief in the night. You know not the time nor the hour. So for today I try to be the best person ever. Don't start worrying about what's coming. If you're trying to be the best person ever today by grace and acceptance to grace, we don't have to worry about any of that stuff. Just be good for today."

16.23 Question: "We should always pray for God's will, and I have a brother who hasn't been to Mass or church for over sixty years. You think twenty, thirty years is a long time. He hasn't been to church for sixty years, and Mother prayed for his conversion for years, and now I pray for his conversion. We should always accept God's will, but conversion is God's will. Why aren't we getting that conversion that we've prayed so hard for?"

Eileen: "Well, keep praying. You can't say God isn't working in his soul. You don't know the secrets of his heart. O.K.? I believe with all my heart, you certainly must go to Mass and go to confession, right? But I know many people that go to Mass and go to confession but maybe they're not going to Heaven, maybe they're going to go to Hell. They're not making good confessions and they're making sacrilegious communions.

"So you have to continue to pray, knowing and trusting that God has heard these prayers and He's working in this man's soul. It might be a deathbed conversion, but don't give up on the prayer, ever. O.K.? Don't ever give up on this prayer. Trust, knowing that God has heard these prayers, and He's working at His own speed. O.K.?"

16.24 Question: "I keep talking to my guardian angel and I don't get a response. I would like to know who he is and to get closer to him. What do I do?"

Eileen: "You have to keep talking to the guardian angel. For years we haven't acknowledged the angel, and now, we're finding out about the angel, so we're saying, 'Come quick. Come quick. Answer me!' No. It's a lifelong process, like falling in love with Jesus. It takes time. You have to be tuned in to him. Not all the saints spoke to their angels. Some did. It's a process, a spiritual growth. We hear a word, we get excited, then we think we're going to jump into it. It takes time. O.K.?"

16.25 Question: "Eileen, when someone dies, does God judge him at that moment?"

Eileen: "In that split second."
"What I'm saying is if someone repented at that moment, is he forgiven then? Does God judge him then, or the whole life span that he lived?"
Eileen: "You mean if it was a deathbed conversion?"
"Let's say if somebody didn't lead a good life but at that minute, that hour of death, he said an act of contrition."
Eileen: "He's saved."
"He's saved?"
Eileen: "Right."
"What I'm trying to say is, how could you say that?"
Eileen: "He said the act of contrition by the grace of God. Remember in Scripture when it talks about the man with the two sons? He killed the fatted calf and everything and his other son said, 'Why? He was a little scoundrel. He was always away from you. I stood by you all the time.' And the father said, 'I'm doing right by you, but my son has returned.' That's what God says.

"But some people will say, 'I'm gonna lead a sinful life. I'm gonna drink. I'm gonna be an adulterer. On my deathbed, I'll be converted.' Says who? Are you going to have the grace to be converted? We can't live that kind of a life because we don't know. It takes grace for conversion.

"Evidently he did something good, or someone was praying for him. He was touched by grace. O.K.?"

16.26 Question: "My husband has a large family and his brother lived with us for nine years, and he cut my husband and three other brothers out of the will. I tried to get the brothers together so there would be peace. Three times I've been there. He goes to church. I told him I think he should make peace with the others. I said, 'I've been here three times now and I'm asking you again, will you please come and make peace with your brother?' And he says, 'Yes,' then he doesn't."

Eileen: "Well, you know you're doing everything you possibly can. Now you have to resort to a deeper power of prayer. 'God, I've done everything possible. He promised, and he broke his promise. I place it in your loving hands, Father, please take take care of this.' O.K.? That's all you can do, honey, otherwise you'll start a war."

16.27 Question: "Eileen, Jesus leads to the Father, Mary leads to Jesus, and how do you feel about sometimes when we're not feeling up to par, we're not sure whether the merits that we offered up, whether we've offered up our sufferings, how do you feel about leaning upon Mary to take whatever we would wish to be offered, when we're not too sure?"

Eileen: "You certainly can do this. Certainly you can. Mary's always ready for us. I have a great love for Mary. I can talk woman talk with Mary. The Lord knows about it already, but when I have something personal, woman talk, I run to Mary. And it's good to run and give her things because she can present them to her son. Remember at the marriage feast at Cana, 'O.K., get busy son, there's no wine here.'

" 'What do you want me to do?'

" 'You know what to do—fill the jugs.'

So He listens to His mother. O.K.? That's good, give them to Mary, she'll bring them to the Son. That's wonderful."

Afterword

Readers who take to Eileen are urged to reread and reread this book, from which they will continue to get light and guidance. Further books of Eileen's teaching will be published by the Meet-the-Father Ministry.

For more information, write for the "Father's Good News Letter."

St. Bede's Publications (P.O.Box 545 Dept EG Petersham, MA 01366) has a brochure of Eileen's tapes: tapes of the first three years of Eileen's monthly services, which are professionally made; and meditative tapes, made by Eileen at home, for those for whom the content is more important than the taping. (These tapes include an occasional barking of one of Eileen's dogs, or the chatter of her parakeets.)

St. Bede's Publications is a work of the contemplative Benedictine St. Scholastica's Priory.

Index